Dr Naomi Fisher is a clinical psychologist who specialises in trauma, autism and alternative education. She is the mother of two and the author of several books on psychology, education and mental health. Her work has featured in *The Psychologist*, *iNews*, *SEN Magazine* and *The Green Parent*, and she has appeared on many podcasts.

Eliza Fricker is an author and illustrator who has written and illustrated two books of her own (*The Family Experience of PDA* and *The Sunday Times* bestseller *Can't Not Won't*) as well has having illustrated several others. She runs a successful illustrated blog about her experiences with her daughter's school-attendance struggles (missingthemark.co.uk) and created the Missing the Mark podcast, an exploration of what happens when a child isn't happy at school. She has spoken at the Rethinking Education conference and gives talks to local authorities on what it's like for families when a child can't attend school.

The
TEENAGER'S
GUIDE TO
BURNOUT

Dr. Naomi Fisher
& Eliza Fricker

ROBINSON

ROBINSON

First published in Great Britain in 2024 by Robinson

5 7 9 10 8 6 4

Copyright © Naomi Fisher and Eliza Fricker, 2024
Illustrations by Eliza Fricker

The moral right of the authors has been asserted.

Important Note
This book is not intended as a substitute for medical advice or treatment.
Any person with a condition requiring medical attention should consult
a qualified medical practitioner or suitable therapist.

In this book, you will read the stories of many different people. Some of these people
are real and they tell the story in their own words. Where this is the case, we've used
their real names and they have checked what we have included. The other stories
are composites. They are all based on real events but not on a real person.
Any resemblance to a real person is accidental.

A CIP catalogue record for this book is available from the British Library.

ISBN: 978-1-47214-938-1

Typeset in Times LT Std by SX Composing DTP, Rayleigh, Essex
Printed and bound in Great Britain by Clays Ltd, Elcograf S.p.A.

Robinson
An imprint of
Little, Brown Book Group
Carmelite House
50 Victoria Embankment
London EC4Y 0DZ

The authorised representative
in the EEA is
Hachette Ireland
8 Castlecourt Centre
Dublin 15, D15 XTP3, Ireland
(email: info@hbgi.ie)

The authorised representative
in the EEA is
Hachette Ireland
8 Castlecourt Centre, Dublin 15,
D15 XTP3, Ireland
(email:info@hbgi.ie)

An Hachette UK Company
www.hachette.co.uk

www.littlebrown.co.uk

Every day we meet families who are realising they
need something different but aren't sure where to start.
This book is dedicated to you.

Contents

Introduction

You've got this book (or someone else has got it for you) because you aren't feeling good. You might be totally lacking in energy and feeling completely flat. Maybe you feel agitated and sort of 'fizzy'. You might be exhausted all the time but be completely unable to sleep. Perhaps you have a strange sort of blank feeling behind your eyes. Stomach aches, headaches or general aches and pains could also be bothering you. To make things worse, you don't really enjoy anything anymore, even things you used to love. Maybe everyone is making you feel really irritable and annoyed.

Or perhaps none of these things apply to you, but you just aren't interested in anything anymore and life has completely lost its sparkle.

You haven't always felt like this. You used to enjoy life and join in with things. You used to get excited about stuff, but now it's like you have nothing left. You are running on empty.

Someone has probably suggested that you are burnt out – or maybe you came up with that idea yourself. It's possible that some of the adults around you are sceptical – they think burnout only happens to adults who carry on in jobs they hate for years on end. They don't think you qualify because you're a young person and you don't have a job. They might not be very nice about it; they may have said you're just being lazy or you need to try harder and pull yourself together. Or, maybe, your parents are agonisingly concerned about you, desperate for you to feel better – and that feels horrible. You know they are worried and you wish they'd just back off.

So what is burnout – and are you burnt out? This book is written to help you find out if that describes you and, if so, what you can do about it. There are degrees of burnout, and, after reading this book, you might decide that, actually, right now you aren't really burnt out but are heading that way. If so, this book has some ideas for how you can stop it from happening in the future.

The book starts by talking about burnout and stress – what these terms mean and how to recognise when they become a problem. It will help you identify some of the ways you get stuck when you're trying to get better and what is and isn't helping. Then, the later part of this book is about what the process of recovery looks like, what you can do at each stage and what the people around you can do to help.

Who We Are

Two of us wrote this book.

Naomi is a clinical psychologist, which means that she specialises in using psychology to help people with their mental health. She had an unusual school journey. She went to eleven different schools, some of which she loved and some of which she hated. Most of the words you'll read here are written by her.

Introduction

Eliza is an illustrator and author of several illustrated books, including *Can't Not Won't*, which is about her daughter's difficulties with school attendance. Her most recent book, *Thumbsucker*, is her rewriting (and redrawing) of her own childhood experiences and some of her own difficulties. All the pictures you'll see here are drawn by her.

1

Burnout and Stress

What is Stress?

Do you ever get stressed? We'd be surprised if you didn't. Neither of us has yet met someone who doesn't get stressed sometimes.

Stress is part of life. Things happen in the world around us that we find challenging and our body responds physically while our brain responds emotionally. We all feel stressed sometimes and more relaxed at other times. You might have felt stressed when you had to take an exam, or when you argue with your friends or your parents.

You feel that stress in your body or in your head. That's because there are stress hormones going through your bloodstream. They are released in response to signals from a part of your brain, which has picked up that a threatening event may be going on. That part of your brain – your amygdala – sends signals to the rest of your body to prepare to protect you. It gets you ready to fight or to get out of the situation.

Being a Stress Detective

What are the signs you notice when you are getting stressed? Lots of people find it hard to see if they are stressed; often, other people notice first! This happens to Naomi a lot. Her family tell her she is being irritable and needs to take some time off, while she thinks she is being perfectly reasonable and they are being more annoying than usual.

Some people notice feelings. Other people notice thoughts. Others notice body sensations. Some people only notice their stress when they first notice they are behaving differently to how they usually do. Maybe they notice that they can't get to sleep at night, or they are waking really early in the mornings. Or they notice they want to eat lots of sweets and chocolate, when usually they eat a healthier diet.

You can get better at noticing the clues telling you that you are stressed. It's like anything else; if you practise, you'll start to notice things you might have missed before. Picking up on signs of stress early on can be helpful because it means you can do something about it before things overwhelm you. Lots of people, particularly adults, ignore their stress until it makes them ill. They try to pretend it isn't there and push it away, and it builds up over time until, suddenly, bang! They can't keep going anymore. You might have seen your parents doing this – you have noticed they are really stressed but they are carrying on as if everything is fine, until suddenly it's not anymore.

Stress is a reaction to the world, and it is one of the ways our bodies get ready to protect themselves. We would feel very stressed if we were about to be attacked by a wild animal and our body's reaction would give us the energy to get away from the animal, or perhaps even fight it off ourselves. This reaction isn't always so useful in the modern world, where we are unlikely to be attacked by a wild animal and we're more likely to be stressed about school work or family.

Naomi always feels stressed before an interview or exam, but she knows now that this reaction will mean that during the exam she won't feel tired, even if she was awake most of the night before. She'll go into the exam and she'll write furiously for the whole time. After the exam is a different story. She'll feel less stressed and then she'll be completely exhausted. She won't even feel able to talk or listen; it'll be like she's run out of charge. Because it has happened lots of times before, she knows now how it goes, and how her brain and body react. This means that she can stop worrying the night before when she can't sleep, because she knows that even if she hardly sleeps a wink, she'll get this rush of energy during the exam that will carry her through.

We all experience stress differently. Some people feel jumpy, irritable and unable to calm down. Others might have meltdowns when they get very stressed, or shout at people.

Being stressed isn't a problem in itself and it's not a feeling we can avoid or even something we should try to avoid. It's just our body's way of responding to challenging circumstances. In fact, it can energise us to face whatever we need to do.

Exercise: Stress Detection

What are the things telling you that you might be feeling stressed?

These could be feelings in your body, emotions or thoughts, or things you notice yourself doing. Some people notice they are stressed because they're waking up early in the morning, for example, or thinking about school work every minute of the day.

You could try completing the table below if you wanted to. You don't have to fill in all the boxes. They are there because everybody notices their stress differently. Some people find it hard to identify their feelings, but do notice their thoughts, while for others, it's all about their bodies. They get headaches, stomach aches or even start vomiting.

	Body	Feelings	Thoughts	Behaviour
When I start to feel stressed, I notice . . .				
When I'm getting more stressed, I notice . . .				
When my stress is really bad, I notice . . .				

The Zone

Over the course of a day, our feelings go up and down. We get stressed about certain things and then we come back to feeling okay. We call this place of feeling okay *the Zone*. When we are in the Zone, we are able to get on with things we enjoy. Feelings come and go, but we don't feel overwhelmed by them. We feel okay. We can interact with other people; we can think about things and our bodies feel okay. It's not that we've become all Zen or are doing anything special, like meditating. We're just able to get on with our lives without it being too distressing.

When something difficult happens and it's a bit too much for us to cope with, we get stressed, and this can take us outside the Zone. Then it might take us a while to get back there.

This is normal. Our feelings come and go. This morning, for example, Naomi had to clean her house because some visitors were coming to look around. They were coming quite early, and she thought she had left enough time to clear up. She was feeling good about how efficient she had been and she was listening to a podcast as she did the cleaning. She was in her Zone.

Five minutes before they were meant to arrive, she discovered her cats had been sick in the front room. Suddenly, she didn't feel so pleased with herself. She had to clean up the cat sick before her guests got there and she had not planned enough time for that. She hates cleaning up cat sick. (Does anyone like cleaning up sick?) She felt her heart racing, her thoughts started buzzing and she felt irritated and frustrated at the cats. Then she felt annoyed with the rest of her family, who weren't helping her with the cleaning, even though she had said they didn't need to stay at home. They were all out doing things they enjoyed, and she was stuck cleaning up cat sick.

She started to feel panicky; did she have enough time? What if it smelled bad and made the whole house stink? She was feeling so stressed, it almost stopped her from being able to clean up the cat sick at all. She just wanted to go out and leave it all there.

Then she decided that she could do it. She took a few deep breaths and had a drink of water. She cleaned up the sick and sprayed some odour remover around and it wasn't as bad as she had thought. The visitors were a bit late anyway and she had a few minutes to spare. In that time, she could feel her body calming down again. Her breathing got slower, her heart rate went back to normal and she started looking forward to the rest of the day. Back in the Zone. She could cope.

Exercise: In the Zone

When you're in your Zone, you feel good enough about yourself and capable of rising to the challenges of life. Difficult things happen, but they don't overwhelm you.

See if you can think of a recent(ish) time when you felt that way. Maybe it was when you were still at primary school and had a teacher whom you liked and who made you feel good about your abilities. Maybe it was a time when you felt things were going okay at home and at school.

Being in the Zone isn't about feeling good all the time, but it is about not feeling overwhelmed by all the things going on in your life. It's feeling you can cope with what the world throws at you. It's about balance.

	Body	Feelings	Thoughts	Behaviour
What do you notice when you're in your Zone?				

Moving in and out of the Zone

Our stress system is meant to be flexible. It energises us when something needs our attention and then, when the crisis is over, our body returns to a calmer state. For Naomi, feeling stressed didn't stop her from being able to get on and clean up, although for a moment it seemed like it might. We move between states of more and less stress all day long. As long as we can do this, there isn't a problem.

Sometimes we don't notice this process happening, but it doesn't always happen with no effort. We make little adjustments to keep ourselves in the Zone all the time. We could decide to take a few moments for ourselves or play a game or go for a run; we might go and get something to eat to help us stay in the Zone. We notice that we are feeling a bit stressed, and we do something to bring ourselves back into the Zone. Having a cup of tea is a very common way in which people do this. Chatting to (the right) other people can really help too. Exercise is a tried-and-tested way to bring yourself back into the Zone, as is contact with water by having a shower or bath. Spending some time by yourself is a good way to keep yourself balanced. If you're really angry with someone, you might choose to step outside for a breather rather than shout at them. We are always coping with stressors and bringing ourselves back to the Zone – when it's going well, you might not even notice yourself doing it.

Exercise: Bringing Yourself Back to the Zone

What are the little ways in which you bring yourself back to the Zone when you're getting stressed?

If you wanted to, you could make a list of the ways in which you bring yourself back to your Zone. These might be things like listening to music, going running or swimming, talking to a friend or hanging upside down from your bed. Some people find walking through sand or grass a helpful way to keep themselves balanced. There might be things you tell yourself – some people find it helpful to repeat mantras to themselves and say things like, 'This too will pass.'

Just as there are things we can do to bring ourselves back into the Zone, some things we do push us further out of the Zone. Sometimes we do things that seem like they will help – like eating loads of sweets – but then make things worse because they have other effects, like you start to feel sick. Or you might text a friend hoping for support, but then that friend is really annoying and it makes you feel worse.

There are also things other people do that can push us further out of the Zone. If you're feeling stressed, it's very unlikely to help if someone shouts at you, for example. Or, if they 'helpfully' remind you of all the things you are stressed about.

Quite often, adults say things they seem to think are helpful but actually aren't. For instance, if you're really stressed about exams, they say, 'These exams are really important, you know.' Or, if you lose something, they say, 'You never look after your stuff properly.' Instead of helping you get back into your Zone, they push you further out and make it harder for you to get back. The stress multiplies, and the Zone feels further and further away.

The Stress Multiplier

Are you someone who gets stressed about feeling stressed? That's a pretty common reaction to feelings. In fact, we'd say we know more people who react like that than those who don't. You start feeling a bit stressed and then you get annoyed about feeling that way, so you tell yourself off or tell the feelings to go away – and before you know it, you're even more stressed.

We call this the Stress Multiplier. There is nothing like adding stress to stress to result in (wait for it) . . . more stress.

Think about it. If you're feeling a bit stressed, and your reaction inside your head is to go – *I shouldn't be feeling like this, I don't want to feel stressed, I hate you stress* – then you are trying to fight stress using stress. It's like trying to put out a fire with more fire.

That is never going to work well. It's like shouting at someone who is upset and angry. We don't know about you, but neither of us has ever met anyone who goes, 'Oh, yeah. Now you've shouted at me I don't feel upset and angry anymore. Thanks.' It doesn't happen.

When you shout at people, they feel angrier and more upset, and they might even shout back at you (making you even more stressed – a double stress multiplier).

It's the same inside your own head. Everyone has stressed feelings sometimes. If you try to make them go away by being annoyed or angry with yourself and your feelings, they will get worse not better.

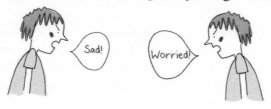

The alternative (and we know it sounds a bit silly) is to remind yourself that stress is part of life and you don't have to fight it. Some people say things to themselves like, I'm having these feelings right now. They will come and go. They won't hurt me. Other people tell themselves, Thanks brain for activating my stress response. I know you're just trying to be helpful. Or, Even though I'm feeling really stressed, I know that I am okay. Others say, This is just how I'm feeling right now.

The trick is to say something to yourself that just accepts how you are feeling, rather than trying to make the feelings go away. You can try out saying different things and experiment with how they make you feel.

Here's a guess as to what you might be thinking – That's stupid. It won't make me feel any better to say something lame like that.

Here's the thing. They aren't meant to make you feel better right away. Yes, really. That's not the aim.

The aim is just to notice how you feel and not to fight your stressed feeling, because that will make the stress grow. It's almost like you are trying to make friends with the stress – Oh, there you are again, you say. I know you can't hurt me and you're trying to help me.

Some people don't like talking to themselves and prefer to think of an image that represents not having to fight with your feelings – by being in a boat on a stormy sea, for example. You can imagine your thoughts and feelings as the waves in the ocean – there's no point in trying to stop the waves. You don't need to fight them and it won't do any good if you do. All you need to do is keep the boat afloat until the water is calmer.

Exercise: Stop the Stress Multiplier

Next time you notice yourself getting a bit stressed, see if you can change what you do next.

Instead of getting annoyed about it, see if you can notice your feelings and say something like, This is just how I'm feeling right now, or, Thanks brain, for trying to keep me safe.

Then just notice how you feel.

It can help to write these things down on your phone or in a notebook because, in the heat of the moment, you are likely to slip back into your usual ways of responding. If you write them down, you can make it easier for yourself to remember them for next time.

Getting Back to the Zone

If you remember (or maybe you don't, that's fine), we said when things are going okay in our life and our feelings are manageable, we are in the Zone. Everything doesn't have to be great, but we're managing. We are able to get on with what we want to do.

When we start to get stressed, we come out of the Zone and life becomes harder to manage. When Naomi is out of the Zone, she starts breaking things and hurting herself by mistake. It's a sure sign that she needs to give herself a short break when she smashes a cup and then cuts herself on the pieces when she tries to clear up the mess. If she doesn't take a break, then usually she breaks something else shortly afterwards (and then gets upset about it).

Coming out of the Zone isn't a problem as long as we can get ourselves back into the Zone again. We need our feelings, even the stressed ones. They are part of what gives us energy and drive. Without our emotions, life would be very . . . placid. Like a calm sea or flat countryside. Okay for a bit, but boring after a while.

Sometimes, however, stress goes on for a really long time. Some people felt stressed all the time during the COVID-19 pandemic. They worried about getting ill, or about their parents losing their jobs. Or they hated being stuck at home. Maybe you've had a situation where you have found life really difficult and it just didn't get easier. Every day, you felt stressed and it didn't stop. When this happens, it can start to feel like your life is on a hamster wheel. Nothing is fun and you can't get off.

Maybe you've had a difficult situation in your family, like your parents arguing or splitting up, and it's made you feel stressed, not just for a short period, but for days and months on end without stopping. You've stopped coming in and out of your Zone, and instead you are just out of it. Stuck. You can imagine the Zone and sort of remember what it felt like to be there, but you can't get there anymore. It's like seeing an earlier, less stressed version of yourself but not being able to remember how to be that person again.

When stress goes on for a really long time, our bodies and brain can get stuck out of the Zone. The stress isn't a useful reaction to the world around us anymore. It doesn't help us get things done. It's just stressful feelings, all the time. It can feel really overwhelming. You might not be able to sleep or want to eat – or you might want to eat all the time and sleep all the time. People react to too much stress in very different ways.

Then something strange happens. If those feelings of stress go on too long, the stress stops feeling like an active, energetic thing and, instead, you start to feel shut down. You might feel really flat, or have no energy left in your body to care about anything anymore. Some people say they feel numb or blank. The Zone seems so far away, you can't even imagine going back there. Your batteries are flat.

This is burnout. You can no longer come back to the Zone, where your body and brain feel okay, and you get stuck in a place of chronic stress. Sometimes, when you're in burnout, you can hardly remember what it felt like to feel okay. When you do feel any feelings, they can feel overwhelming and painful, and you'd rather stay feeling numb.

A Quick Recap

We've covered a lot of ground in this chapter, so here's a recap to make sure we all know where we are. You might want to use this section to remind you what the chapter was about later on. You can skip this part if you like. In fact, you can skip any part that doesn't feel quite right for you. This book is for you, and it's up to you which parts you read and try out and in what order.

We all experience stress in our lives and that is part of being human. When we are able to manage the amount of stress each day and still feel okay, we call this being in the Zone. We are all making little adjustments to keep ourselves in the Zone all the time. We feel a bit stressed for a while, and then we feel less stressed.

When we are in a highly stressful situation for a long time, we don't get the chance to get back into our Zone. It starts to feel normal to feel stressed all the time. At first, that stress can feel activating and energetic. You might feel buzzy all the time or find it impossible to sleep. If that goes on for too long, however, you run out of juice. You start to feel flat and low in energy, and that is burnout. It can feel totally impossible for things to go back to how they were before that happened.

Burnout happens because the demands of the world around you have exceeded your capacity to cope with them for a long period of time. It is your body and brain's way of saying STOP.

2

The Burnout Traps

Burnout is Full of Traps

Okay, so we've talked about what burnout is and how it happens. We've talked about how stress is useful in small doses, but when it goes on for too long you can get stuck feeling stressed and you can't get back to feeling okay. When you've been stressed for too long, it's like your body runs out of energy, and instead of the stress making you feel agitated and edgy, it makes you feel flat and exhausted. It's like running out of fuel.

Now we're going to talk about what happens when you are actually in burnout. At this point, you have very little energy. Nothing feels fun or interesting anymore. It can feel like you're dragging yourself through life.

Then, to make things worse, lots of people get stuck in vicious cycles. What does this mean? A vicious cycle is when you feel a certain way, so you do something about it – and what you do makes you feel worse, not better. What you did probably seemed like a good idea at the time, but in the long term it makes things worse. Even though that was not your aim at all.

We call these the **Burnout Traps.** All the things you do to try and help you feel better result in you feeling worse and more trapped than before.

It's like trying to dig your way out of a hole with a spade. The more you dig, the bigger the hole gets and the deeper down you go. When you're feeling burnt out, those traps are everywhere and you can get stuck. Whatever you do to try and make things better ends up making things worse. You (and the people around you) can be putting in loads of effort to stay exactly where you are, or even to get deeper into the hole.

Burnout traps tend to have three themes.

Trap 1: Exhaustion and Lethargy

This one probably doesn't need any description. You know what this means. However, you might not have thought about some of the ways that it shows up. Exhaustion isn't just about feeling tired – and strangely, you can feel totally exhausted but be unable to sleep.

Perhaps you feel lethargic all the time, or apathetic about doing anything. It might seem just too much to have a shower or change your clothes, even if you start to smell. Even going to the kitchen feels like it's too much. Then you can get into vicious loops because when you don't wash, it feels horrible, and when you can't go to the kitchen, you can't get food that you want – so you feel worse and worse, and less and less energetic. Changing things around you becomes a huge step.

You probably also feel fatigued. Fatigue is different to normal tiredness because it's not solved by sleep or rest. When you are fatigued you just feel drained, or your muscles might ache. Maybe you have trouble thinking or concentrating – sometimes people call this 'brain fog'; like your brain is being filled with cotton wool.

The type of exhaustion you have when you are burnt out often doesn't respond well to rest if you think of rest as 'doing nothing'. You can rest all day and still feel just as tired at the end of the day as you did at the start. So you can get stuck in another trap – you rest because you feel tired, but the resting doesn't help the tiredness and makes you feel bored and lethargic, because you aren't doing anything interesting.

Burnout is full of traps and vicious cycles. You do something because you are feeling so terrible, and then the thing you do makes you feel more terrible. You stay in bed all day because you are so worn out and bored by everything in life, and then staying in bed is boring and makes you feel even more worn out. The things you do to try and make you feel better, end up with you feeling worse.

Trap 2: Seeing the Negative in Everything

When you're burnt out, it's hard to feel positive. You start to put a negative spin on absolutely everything. It's like having mud-covered spectacles – the opposite of rose-tinted ones. No matter what happens, you see the worst side of things. Someone makes you a cake to try and cheer you up, and all you can think about is that they put pink icing on it and you hate pink.

This is often particularly intense when it comes to your family or the people you live with. You might find your parents extremely annoying and feel angry with them almost all the time. Little things they do, like humming while they drive, asking you how you are or moving your bag when you leave it in the hall, become really irritating. You notice those things more than before. Everyone and everything makes you feel worse.

These negative feelings can mean that you start to push away the people you love. It's annoying when adults are hanging around asking questions or trying to help, so you are horrible to them and they go away. Then you start to feel bad about how you have made them feel, which makes you feel worse – it's one of those traps again. Over time, other people might start to avoid asking you how you are or trying to help, and then you feel worse than before because it feels like no one cares.

Didn't we say burnout is full of traps?

Trap 3: Feeling Like You Can't Do Anything Well

This is a weird one, but there's a lot of evidence that people feel better about themselves when they feel they can do things well. Think about what it feels like when you're playing a video game, or writing a story, or playing a sport or musical instrument and you are doing it well. That feeling of being good at something, of doing it well, is really important. Another important feeling is the one you have when you become more skilled at things. From a psychological perspective, it doesn't matter too much what that thing actually is; it's the sense you are improving and seeing the results of your efforts that matters.

Where do you get this feeling of being able to do something well? Some teenagers find it in video games, others in sports or music. Some find it in writing stories, skateboarding or making digital art.

If you've been working hard at school for a long time and not doing well or doing well but feeling that you are not doing well enough, then it's not surprising if you start to feel that you aren't capable. You might have worked really hard and then not got the exam results you were hoping for, or you put a lot of effort into a project your teacher said wasn't good enough or which didn't get a good mark.

Lots of people don't feel good about themselves at school but they are able to do things well outside school – when they are playing sport, or *Dungeons and Dragons*, or practising a musical instrument, for example. Or even just hanging out with their friends and feeling appreciated by them.

Naomi really likes playing board games online. She enjoys games of strategy, like *Le Havre*, *Agricola* and *Evolution*, and trains against the AI to improve her skills before playing against a real person. At the start, she is totally incompetent and loses, even to the easiest AI, but over time she improves and she can upgrade the AI. It's fun to feel a sense of getting better and it doesn't really matter if she wins or loses the games. Once she has learnt how to beat the hardest AI, it's not so much fun anymore, particularly if no one else will play with her. She often seeks out new games she doesn't know, to get that feeling of improving at something.

When someone goes into burnout, the feeling of being not good at things spreads to everything. Before, maybe you used to feel like that just with school work or a particular subject at school, but now everything feels that way. There is no point in doing anything, you say to yourself, and the future will be just as hopeless as you feel right now.

These feelings get you into another trap. You feel you are no good at anything and think there's no point in trying, so you don't try anything new or put in any effort. That means you don't get a chance to improve at anything – and you don't get the stimulation of improving at something you enjoy. And that means life is more boring and feels even more pointless. There are more traps to fall into everywhere you look.

Exercise: Where Are You Stuck?

A burnout trap happens when what you are doing to try and feel better actually makes you feel worse in the long term. The more effort you put into it, the more stuck you get – because your efforts only help in the short term.

You are almost certainly stuck in some burnout traps but they aren't always easy to see when you're in them.

Sometimes it's easier to see other people's traps. Here are some examples of traps people get stuck in. Can you identify any traps of your own? You can fill them in in the spaces provided if you feel like it.

The Teenager's Guide to Burnout

How I'm Feeling	What I Do	Short-term Effect	Long-term Effect
Lethargic	Cancel meeting up with friends and going out	Relief that I won't have to make the effort	Feel more bored and lethargic
Angry	Shout at my dad when he comes into my room	Dad goes away and gets out of my space	Feel guilty and now Dad is upset
I can't do anything	Stop working on my coding project	Less frustrated because it was hard work doing the coding	I feel it's true, I really can't do anything
Sad and lonely	Shut myself in my bedroom and stop responding to my friends	It doesn't feel as bad when no one can see me and I don't have to make the effort	My friends stop getting in touch and I feel lonelier

A Quick Recap

We've talked about lots of different things in this chapter and you might be finding it hard to hold all of it in your head. It's often a struggle for people with burnout to remember things or to keep track of what they are reading. This is a brief reminder of what burnout traps look like.

'Burnout traps' is a name for the vicious cycles lots of people get stuck in. These psychological traps are a bit like Chinese finger traps – those ones where you put your finger in, and the harder you try to pull your finger out, the more stuck it gets.

With burnout traps, the things you are doing to try to feel better end up making you feel worse. For example, you feel bored and lethargic, so you cancel going out with your friend and stay in bed instead, leaving you feeling even more bored and lethargic. Then you do even less, and before you know it you're in a downward spiral. The things you are doing to help yourself end up making you feel worse. It's like you are digging yourself into a bigger hole while trying to get out.

3

School Burnout

Burnout Doesn't Mean There is Anything Wrong with You

We've been listing all the ways in which you could experience burnout and how you might have ended up there. But now you're worried about what this all means for you and those around you. Perhaps you're worried you are really unwell and that you aren't going to get better. We're going to turn that around and say, you know what . . . ?

There's nothing wrong with you.

Really. You aren't ill or broken or damaged. It's not that you're not trying hard enough, or you're not resilient or whatever else people have been saying. Your body and brain are simply saying ENOUGH. You have been pushing yourself through stress and pressure for a long time, and your body has probably been sending you lots of little warning signals you have ignored and pushed through (or other people have made you push through). Your body is saying this cannot carry on, and it is going to make sure that, this time, you, and everyone else, listens.

Your body is working exactly as it is meant to.

Burnout is how your body and brain react to chronic stress and pressure. It's about you responding to what has happened to you. It's your body saying, 'NO MORE, STOP, THAT'S ENOUGH.' Loudly and clearly, so you can't ignore it.

Sceptical? It's not just us who say this. The World Health Organization (WHO) (a huge international organisation that, among other things, publishes manuals on medical diseases and disorders) says burnout is an 'occupational phenomenon', not a medical problem.

What this means that it's something that happens when the demands of what a person does every day become too much for them, over a long period of time. It's a natural reaction to circumstances. It's your body's automatic cut-out mechanism, designed to keep you alive and kicking.

The WHO says 'occupational' because they think burnout is caused by the stress adults feel about work, but there's no reason why burnout has to be only from a job. It can be from anything you have to do over an extended period of time that puts you under stress, including school and all the other things that have happened to you in your life.

Can School Cause Burnout?

School is one of the things teenagers tell us causes them intense stress – but they often feel really bad about this. After all, (nearly) everyone goes to school, right? Everyone else seems to manage okay, or at least they look as if they are managing okay. It's easy to think the problem must be you, and sometimes adults will say things suggesting this. They'll say, 'Maybe you could try a bit harder' or 'What exactly *is* the problem?' and you just don't know what to say.

If you are someone who finds school really stressful and difficult, or who hasn't been going to school for a while, you have probably discovered there are lots of people ready to tell you about the benefits of school. They will explain to you why it isn't really as bad as you think, or why it's really important for your future and everyone just has to get through it. They might say annoyingly chirpy things like, 'If you want to change the way the world works, you'll need to get some qualifications first!' They might say you look perfectly fine when you're there, so they don't understand what the problem is.

People have perhaps told you that school is compulsory and your parents could go to prison if you don't keep going. This isn't actually true in most countries of the world. Education is compulsory and your parents must make sure you are getting an education, but that doesn't have to mean school. School is only one way to get an education.

Sometimes adults seem to think that all they need to do is explain to you why you are wrong to feel the way you do, and – pouf – you'll feel better, go back to school and all will be well.

This book is different. That's because we think you don't need to be told about all the positive things about school and how important it is. We think there's a very good chance you know all those things and it hasn't helped. And if you don't know those things, there will be no shortage of people who will tell you. We think (and know from experience) that when you are in burnout, being told all the reasons why you shouldn't feel as bad as you do and should just get on with your life doesn't help and can make you feel worse.

For that reason, we're going to spend some time thinking about why school feels so stressful and difficult for you. Perhaps the most important thing to start with is that it is not just you who feels this way. You may not know other people who are burnt out by school, but we have met and heard about thousands of them. You aren't alone.

An Alien Arrives

Imagine if aliens came down and landed on Earth, and they landed next to a school. They'd see all the kids dressed the same (in schools with uniforms), sitting in rows and putting their hand up to speak. They'd see signs saying things like, 'No running in the corridors' and they'd see groups of kids walking from room to room, then sitting down and listening to adults talking and then writing down things on pieces of paper. They'd see kids getting into trouble if they don't do what they are told and being made to sit in more desks in silence for longer. They'd see certain times of the day when all the kids come out and there is loads of action for a short period, and then everyone stands in lines and go back into the rooms where they sit at tables. What would the aliens make of it all, we wonder.

They might think, this is a pretty weird thing for this species to do with their young. They'd be right.

We are all so used to school that we don't think much about how strange it really is. We just think that school is like it is, and it has to be like that and always will be like that. But school isn't the only way to learn – and the way your school is isn't the only way a school can be.

When Naomi was growing up, her parents moved around the world and she went with them. That means she went to many different schools. All of them had broadly similar ideas about what a school should be like. Teacher at the front, kids at desks or tables. They all followed a curriculum, although they all followed different curricula and thought different things were important. They all made the kids write things down and do homework.

But apart from that, they had other ideas that were quite different. The schools in England had uniforms and they thought those were very important. One school even measured the girls' skirts to make sure they weren't too long or too short (apparently, long skirts are a trip hazard on the stairs. Who knew?). Other schools had no uniform at all, and hardly anyone wore skirts. Jeans worked fine. The relationships between the students and teachers were different too. In some schools, the teachers were really friendly and were called by their first names; in others, they hardly smiled and were called Sir or Miss.

They taught different things at different times. In the Steiner school Naomi attended, the kids did lots of art and knitting and didn't start learning to read until they were seven or eight. But in the primary school she went to in Bristol, the very first thing everyone did when they were five was sit cross-legged on the carpet and start to learn to read.

By moving around to so many schools, Naomi learnt that just because a school says something has to be a certain way doesn't mean it must be like that. Something one school thinks is really important – like wearing a tie or using a fountain pen or standing up when the teacher comes into the room – another school doesn't even mention. Everyone wears what they want and writes with a ballpoint pen (and even chooses what colour ink they write in) and the world does not fall apart.

You Look Fine to Me

You've probably already identified that there are many things about school that don't work well for you. You might, however, have thought that the real problem is you. Because everyone seems to go to school, and most people appear to just 'get on with it', when kids find school really doesn't work for them, they often think it must be their fault. Sometimes, the adults imply it's their fault too. They say things like, 'Can't you just try harder?' or 'You look fine once you're here.'

Naomi really hated one of her schools. The other kids thought she was weird, the work was boring, there were nine forms in each year group and she felt completely anonymous. She went from really liking her previous school to absolutely hating the new one. It made her feel ill. She told one of the teachers about it. The teacher said, 'I saw you yesterday with a group of girls. You looked fine.' Naomi said nothing. She knew there was no point. But what she thought was, I have to look fine. I'm in the middle of a huge school and no one likes me. I have to try to blend in. What other option is there? It's not like I'm going to walk around crying.

That was when Naomi realised those teachers were not going to be able to help. They couldn't see the problem at all. They just thought she was making a fuss about nothing because they couldn't see the problem from Naomi's point of view. What you can see of people from the outside isn't the same as how they feel on the inside.

Why is School so Hard for Me?

School works in a certain way. Teachers have a curriculum they have to teach to the kids. A curriculum is basically a list of stuff kids should know. In one year, it might be the ancient Egyptians, another year it's the Romans. Then there are fractions and decimals and reading Shakespeare. The kids have to try and learn it as best they can, and then they are asked to show what they have learnt. The curriculum is designed by people who never meet any of the students. They've decided that this is what everyone should learn without knowing them.

Being successful at school means remembering what you've been taught and showing that to teachers and in exams. The teacher and the examiner are the ones who decide whether what you remember is the right stuff. You might remember lots of stuff about William the Conqueror, but if you're being asked about Henry VIII, that's essentially useless.

At the end of school, you take exams that are all about how much you can remember – you sit in a room with lots of other people and you're not allowed to look anything up or ask questions. Yet, in real life, you can pretty well always look something up, ask someone else what they think or check it on your phone.

School is a competition and it's not a competition everyone can win. You get compared against other people all the time. 'Doing well' means doing better than other people. Many school exams award marks in percentages. About 30% of those who take the exam will always fail, no matter how hard they work. If everyone does really well, they'll say it's too easy and they'll change the marks so that some people still fail – and make the exam harder next time.

Schools are standardised – students of the same age are expected to learn the same thing. Each year, you move up a class and now there is a new curriculum to learn. For some people, this means that the work is too easy and they are bored. For others, it's too hard and they feel they never quite understand before moving on to the next thing. It's like a train that just keeps going, even though you would really like to stop at the station for a bit to work out where you are. If you're someone who is happier with those younger or older than yourself – or who prefers to spend time by yourself – then you're in a sticky position.

People aren't standardised. Kids learn things at different rates. Some babies learn to walk and talk much more quickly than others, and this doesn't mean they end up better at walking and talking in the long run. Some kids learn to read really quickly when they are young – some even manage to teach themselves just from being read to – while others take a lot longer. Some people are really good at things like art and want to spend all their time doing this. Eliza was like that at school, while Naomi wanted to spend all her time reading and making friendship bracelets under the desk. People are very different, no matter what age they are.

This creates a problem. School is standardised and people aren't. School tries to push people through a standardised process, but that just doesn't work for lots of people. They feel they have to squash parts of themselves in order to fit into the system.

Exercise: You and School

What do/did you like about school (now or in the past)?

What do/did you find difficult about it?

Have there been times when it was better or worse?

What made the difference?

Things Everyone Tells You About School
(That Might Not be True)

Wait a minute, you might be thinking. Surely I have to go to school if I want to learn and do well in the future?

One of the most important ways in which schools work is that they convince everyone that going to school is the only way to learn. They convince them so well that even the people for whom school really doesn't work are often convinced school is really important and the only option. Sometimes, it's the people who did worst at school themselves who are most convinced that it's absolutely essential and that children must go, no matter how much they hate it.

It's a bit like propaganda. Propaganda is a form of advertising often used by governments during wartime to persuade people the war is a good idea and that they should keep supporting the government and join the army. You might have seen some propaganda posters from both world wars saying things like, 'Your Country Needs You' or 'Dig For Victory'.

School propaganda tells you that school is essential and that everyone loves school. This starts early – when you were little you might have been read some of those books aimed at little kids all about how exciting school will be. Topsy and Tim, or Peppa Pig, or Spot the Dog go to school and have a lovely time.

As you get older, school propaganda gets a bit more complex. Adults tell kids that if they don't go to school, they'll never pass their exams or amount to anything. They might even tell you that going every day is essential if you're going to be a future success.

We wonder if your school has posters up telling you how important school is. Most schools we visit do. There are pictures of sad, bored people, saying they wish they'd attended more school and done better in their exams, or posters telling you that if you're late to school for five minutes each day that adds up to lots and lots of learning over the course of a year (even though that makes no sense at all, because being five minutes late means you miss registration, where no one is learning anything. It's annoying for the school, but it doesn't mean you're doomed to a life of educational failure).

These posters can sometimes make you scared that if you leave, your life will be over – so even when it's terrible, you keep going. You keep going even though you are stressed all the time, and then you start to feel burnt out.

In fact, there are many things you might have been told about school that aren't true. We've made a table of some of the most common school myths we've heard – and the truth.

School Myth	Truth
You have to do well at school in order to succeed in life.	Many people do badly at school and then find something they love later and become very successful.
Attending school every day is essential for your future.	The school building is not magic. Attending school every day will not in itself make any difference to your future. It's what you are doing at school that counts, and if you aren't learning there, then being there will make no difference.
If you are twelve minutes late to school every day, that adds up to an hour's lost learning every week and a day every half term.	You can't break down learning into minutes. In some minutes you will learn lots, in others nothing. Missing the first twelve minutes of school probably means missing registration and maybe some of assembly – not much 'learning' there.

In the real world, there are no excuses. We won't listen when you tell us why you couldn't do your homework.	In the real world. if something happens and you can't meet a deadline, you can ask for help or negotiate an extension.
Going to school is the only way to learn.	People learn very effectively out of school. Adults do it all the time. There are kids who don't go to school who go on to take exams and go to university.
Learning isn't meant to be fun.	When you are interested, learning is fun. Even really hard stuff can be fun.
You have to do all the subjects to get an all-round education.	There is nothing special about the subjects taught in school. They are arbitrary. Countries don't even agree on what subjects kids should study. 'All-round' is a made-up concept. Why do schools make you study geography but not psychology, for example?
You have to pass exams when everyone else does in order to go to college.	There are many different ways into college and university. Exams can be taken at different ages or not at all. Some colleges will take you with no qualifications.
You have to get used to doing things you don't like, as you'll need this skill when you are an adult.	You may have to do some things you don't like as an adult. But there will often be reasons for those things. For example, you might do a job you don't like for the money. That is different to school, where you have no choice.
If you miss school, you'll get behind and you'll never catch up.	If you miss school, you'll miss whatever they taught that day or week. You will probably be able to catch that up if you are motivated by using the textbook or by asking someone to explain it to you. School is not a very efficient way to cover information. Some people miss a lot of school and still manage to pass exams (Naomi was like this).
Schools are where learning happens most efficiently.	Schools are often an inefficient way to learn. Out of school, you can learn many more things and often more effectively.
The things you learn at school are more important than things you learn out of school.	The things you learn because you are interested and you enjoy them are likely to be the most important for your future life.

School is the only way to get an education.	There are many ways to get an education and school is only one of them.
Young people have to be made to learn or they'd never do anything hard.	Young people who have never been to school learn lots of things because they want to. They often choose really hard things, like Mandarin Chinese or coding. Making people do things often makes them want to do that thing less.
School is the best place for everyone.	School works for some people and doesn't work for others. If it really doesn't work, it's not the best place for anyone to be.
Doing well in life is about establishing good habits. You need to go to school every day and dress smartly in order to get in the habit for adulthood.	Life is about a lot more than habits. You may do many things in the future and lots of them will not be anything like a school day. You might work at a job with shifts, you might do a job (like working in a garage) where clothes are practical rather than smart, or you might have children and take time off work to look after them. You need to be able to adapt to different situations and make decisions for yourself.
If we let you off, we're letting you down. (Usually used to justify a punishment.)	Trying to understand why someone has behaved the way they did and not punishing them for that isn't letting them down. It's how most compassionate humans interact with one another.

Many people do not do well at school or find school really hard. They go on to do other things and lead interesting lives. We asked some real people who didn't thrive at school how life had turned out for them. Their stories are in boxes so you can see clearly what they said.

Jonny's Story

I was raised in a single-parent family and went to a big comprehensive school. My mum got ill with leukaemia when I was thirteen. My brother and I got split up and had to live at different friends' houses for a while, only seeing each other at school. Then Mum moved back into the house but was dying in the back room. We had some home-help workers who came to help with chores. I was embarrassed when friends would knock round and her wig was on the stairs or she was in a wheelchair. I didn't speak to anyone at school about my situation, although the teachers knew.

My mum died when I was fifteen and my brother was eighteen. Because he was eighteen, we could stay in the house and he became my legal guardian. I was in detention because I was late every day. My brother was young to take on so much responsibility so his reaction was to go out drinking and fighting. I did work experience at a record shop and immersed myself in music and DJing. At school I got all Cs and Ds but it was enough to go to college.

From the record shop, I saw older kids go to college, get a student loan and then get out of town. This was my escape route. I did media studies and English language at college and then went on to do a music production diploma. I lasted a year and dropped out. From that point I got part-time jobs and started to put on my own events.

Today, I run a brand called Sports Banger, which just celebrated its tenth birthday. It's an eccentric UK fashion house. We make T-shirts, fashion pieces, put on raves, release records, publish books. We do whatever we want. I'm lucky I've been able to tell my story through my T-shirts and other work. Everything is united in the spirit of do-it-yourself. The work deals with politics and issues surrounding welfare and community. Our motto is start where you are, use what you've got, do what you can.

I'd like to tell today's teenagers that we've got loads on our hands to get creative with and excited or angry about. Art is so powerful. Clothing is powerful. Raving is political. Find whatever you believe in and go for it. Have fun and don't forget to say what you mean.

Jonny Banger, owner of Sports Banger

The Way School Makes You Feel

One problem with school, as you've probably worked out for yourself, is that many kids find it stressful and it makes them unhappy. Some people dislike being in large groups of other people their age all day. They dislike being made to do things they don't want to do. They dislike being away from home and their families. They don't like the way school smells and sounds. Some people find the playground hectic and confusing.

And many people really don't like the way schools control behaviour and punish young people who don't follow the rules. In fact, it scares them.

Many schools have particular ways they want young people to behave. These vary – some schools are very strict and will allow no talking in the corridors and even tell kids they have to follow the teacher with their eyes all the time. There are even schools that have an acronym for this, SLANT. It stands for Sit up, Listen, Ask and

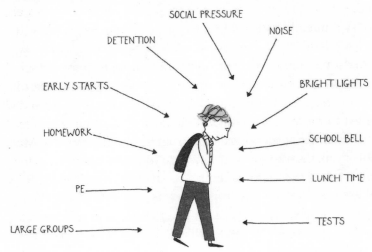

SOCIAL PRESSURE

NOISE

DETENTION

EARLY STARTS

BRIGHT LIGHTS

HOMEWORK

SCHOOL BELL

LUNCH TIME

PE

LARGE GROUPS

TESTS

Answer Questions, Nod your head, Track the speaker. It comes from a book called *Teach Like a Champion* by Doug Lemov. Lemov says this behaviour helps kids pay attention. However, it's not true that sitting up and nodding helps everyone pay attention. Some people pay attention best when bouncing on a trampoline or lying down on the floor with their eyes closed, or even doing something else with their hands. Kids who track the teacher and nod their heads might look like they are paying attention and learning, but even though you can try to control someone's body, you can't control what is going on in their head.

Not all schools tell you how to move your eyes and head, but they still have rules enforcing things like attending classes you find boring or doing homework you find pointless. They might even have rules about when you can go to the toilet or drink water. They make you spend all your time with people the same age as you. They rarely have places where you can do the things you enjoy or learn about things that interest you.

Schools sometimes say these rules are to help everyone learn, but in reality it seems more likely they are about how to control large groups of teenagers who don't necessarily want to be there and who don't get to make many of their own decisions about their life. It's very unusual for a school to let kids choose what they do. Mostly, schools think they know what kids should be doing, and it is the job of kids to do it without making a fuss. If that doesn't work for you – well, that's when the control comes in.

Many people don't respond well to lots of rules and feeling controlled. Naomi absolutely hates being controlled. She went to a conference recently. She had paid to attend it and had travelled across Europe to be there. When she got there, however, Naomi discovered the organisers were checking her in and out of each session with an app that gave her points if she attended the 'right' meetings. She was annoyed. She didn't want to be tracked and she immediately started working out ways to hack the system. Now she felt forced to go to the sessions, she wanted the points without attending them. She realised that as long as she checked in, it didn't matter if she checked out. So she checked in, then walked out and attended other sessions she hadn't checked in to or chatted with other people attending the conference. When she felt they were forcing her to attend particular sessions, she didn't want to go anymore. Force has that effect on a lot of people. Humans don't like being made to do things.

Lots of kids don't like being controlled. It makes them feel resentful and angry. When people feel angry, they show it in different ways – not just through talking, but often through how they behave. I'll bet you know many ways in which your parents or other adults behave differently when they are angry, even when they try to hide it.

Sometimes, when kids get angry and show it through their behaviour, everyone focuses on the kids' behaviour rather than how they feel. They say the behaviour is unacceptable and must change. Schools do things like putting kids on report, sending them to isolation, putting them in detention or giving them lines. They also sometimes use what they call 'positive reinforcement', which means giving you awards or prizes if you do what they want. Some of these things may have happened to you.

None of these things address the reason for a person's behaviour. Instead, they just try to get the person themselves to change. They work by trying to make you unhappy when you don't do what they want, or happy when you do.

If you are clear-sighted enough that you refuse to be controlled in this way, you might find yourself suspended or excluded. Some people are more sensitive to control than others and mind it more. Generally, if someone keeps refusing to be controlled, then some schools will introduce more serious consequences and the person gets more and more unhappy.

Exercise: Under Control?

This exercise is a chance to reflect on what it's like for you when other people try to make you do things. The first step is to notice that it's happening, so you can make a choice for yourself about how you want to respond. Sometimes, you will really have no choice, but at other times you may have some options.

What are the ways in which people try to make you do things?

How do you feel when someone tries to make you do something you don't want to do?

How does it make you feel inside?

What do you do about it?

Does that help?

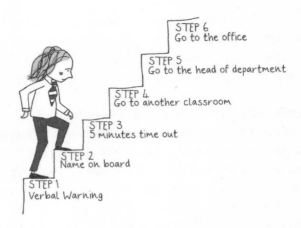

Katy's Story

I was academically clever and liked learning but I was not like everyone else and was bullied. I stuck to the learning disability room after that, so no one would beat me up. I used to do the same jigsaw of the British Isles over and over in that room. I got to school early and avoided the bus, I joined a club so I could leave late.

I was hung from a coat hook by bullies and they threatened anyone who didn't hit me. This incident meant I was kept at home for three days. I had asthma, which gave me time off; respite, I suppose.

I wanted to apply to Cambridge and Oxford but school told me I wouldn't get in. I was also told I 'would make a good prison warder', with a predicted C grade, even though I was an A-grade student. So I took a year out, went to Goldsmiths and then reapplied to my preferred universities and got in. My academic drive is learning and I'm not career-driven; I loved the research.

I then worked for a national newspaper until I was made redundant, so I went to Bristol to study archaeology for screen and then worked in TV as a development producer. But there was a lot of undermining, a lack of trust and belief, and eventually I snapped and walked out. I quit. I was burnt out.

So I went back to learning. I did another Master's degree in development and moved to Kenya. I knew I wanted to learn everything about a culture and this was it.

There is so much pressure on teenagers to know what they want to do, but I think doing lots of things should not be seen as a failure but a badge of honour. I knew early on I didn't fit, so I'm playing to my own tune. I need my own autonomy and sense of identity.

Katy Barnes, owner of a houseplant and
homeware company, Kenya

A Quick Recap

If you've had trouble at school, or trouble going to school, then you may have been told that the problem is you. You might even think that it's all your fault; you should try harder to be more like everyone else. Maybe you think there's something wrong with you. Everyone seems to think that school must be in the right.

You aren't alone. Lots of teenagers find school very stressful and difficult, not just because of the academic pressure but because of the way they are expected to behave and how they are controlled. Some of them get into trouble a lot or worry about getting into trouble a lot. Adults often respond to this by telling kids that if they don't do well at school, their whole life will be blighted. Unsurprisingly, this doesn't help anyone to like school more and it makes lots of teenagers feel even worse. They feel that not only are things bad now, but they won't have a future either.

This doesn't have to be the case. There are other ways to learn apart from school, and lots of people who weren't successful at school go on to lead interesting and fulfilling lives. School is not the only way to learn.

4

A Recipe for Burnout

Learning is Everywhere (Not Just at School)

When you're burnt out, it's common to feel that you don't want to learn anything new and everything is boring. You feel you're just going through the motions.

There's a strange thing about learning. Learning is interesting when you can choose what you learn about. It's interesting when you feel in control of what you are learning. It's stimulating when you feel you are getting better at something.

It isn't the same when you are being made to do it. If you have no choice about what you are learning, it immediately makes the learning less interesting, as if by magic. Even when it's the same thing you're learning about. A book you choose to read (and know you can stop reading) often feels much more interesting than a book you are obliged to read.

Many teenagers tell me they don't get much choice about what they learn, either inside or outside school. They can't choose to really focus on learning about *Dungeons and Dragons*, or bouldering, or Japanese anime, or carpentry or making podcasts because people say that's not as important as the subjects they have to learn for exams.

Here's the thing. All of these things are learning, and some of them may be much more important in your future life than the stuff you have to learn for exams. You might need to pass some exams in order to do the things you want to do in the future, but that doesn't mean that what you learn for exams is more important than everything else.

It makes a big difference to learning when you know you're going to be tested on it. Knowing they will be tested immediately makes most people anxious about learning – but it also affects your behaviour in other ways you might not have even noticed.

Research shows that when people know they'll be tested on their learning, they tend to choose the easiest option, if a choice is available. That makes sense. You want to maximise your chances of getting the best mark. Whereas if you are learning for your own purposes or for interest, then you're more likely to choose something more challenging and, often, more stimulating.

Naomi did this when she was at school. When she had to choose which exams she would take, she knew she would probably get an A in Music, because she already played two musical instruments. Unfortunately, she really didn't like school music. It was boring and she didn't like the teacher. She would have preferred to do Design

Tech or Art but she wasn't as sure that she'd get an A for those. She was much less skilled at them and had more to learn. She chose Music. She spent two years being bored and she got an A at the end. She stopped doing Art and Design Tech completely. When everything is tested and graded, those sorts of choices make sense. But if Naomi's aim had been learning new things, then Music was the wrong thing to choose. She didn't learn much at all.

Because many schools don't allow kids many choices about what they learn, learning immediately becomes harder and more boring. And because of that, kids become disruptive or refuse to do what they are told. And then, adults get upset about that; they become more controlling and that makes everything worse.

It's another of those vicious cycles.

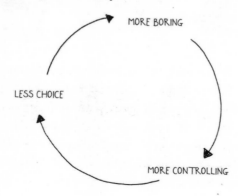

There are lots of different ways to learn, and you are probably using some of them already. Maybe you're watching a YouTube video and they mention something that interests you, so you go and look it up. Maybe you read books about topics that interest you or you have conversations with people who know more about a subject than you do. Maybe you quiz yourself on capitals and flags of the world or write quizzes for other people on topics you know a lot about. Maybe you research how to play a game better by finding walkthroughs and guides. All of these things are learning. Winstan, whose story is told below, found his career through skateboarding, even though he wasn't allowed to bring his skateboard to school.

Winstan's story

I really enjoyed secondary school and was gutted when it ended. I had no idea of what to do next after so many great experiences. I had lots of friends, some of them I carried over from primary school. Now that tight crew was kinda disbanded except for my skateboarding friends who continued with me. At the time, in 1985, school was very different. Some of the teachers had it in for me, but there were good teachers too.

There were also lots of strange rules. It wasn't until I started skateboarding to school that I found out we weren't allowed to skate in school, or even bring a skateboard to school. My board got confiscated a few times. History lessons never reflected my culture as an African Caribbean. My English teacher, who I didn't get on with, made sure I never got the options I wanted for the final two years, and Media Studies was one of them. It didn't go so well with my exam grades, but I still completed school in 1990.

When I finished school, skateboarding was my main thing. I was deep into the scene and got to know everyone in lots of skate spots across London. In 1990, I became a skateboarding amateur for a US company called Blind Skateboards. They were making their first videos and the team wanted me to take them to different spots across London. That was my first insight into how to make a skateboarding video and it had a big influence on me.

An opportunity arose when Tim Leighton-Boyce, a fantastic mentor/friend and brilliant photographer, told me about a new video magazine called *411* from the US. It was in its beginning stages. The idea was to send cameras around the globe so that each skateboarding scene could document itself.

Tim knew that I knew everybody and gave me the camera to film all I could, and for others to film me. I would pass the camera on to other friends and they would pass it back to me. The tapes would get filled and Tim would post it to the States. It was pure learning-as-I-went-along; that was my first true hands-on experience.

I loved it and I eventually bought my own camera in 1997 and began documenting skateboarding for myself. I decided I wanted to go beyond skateboarding filmmaking, so I went to college to do a one-year City & Guilds photography course, then the next year a film and video course.

In 1999, I began to work on short films and music videos, drama movies and TV series as a key camera grip, then I moved into cinematography in 2003 from shooting music videos. In 2005, I released my first skateboarding documentary feature film *Rollin' Through the Decades*. From then on, I continued making independent films and freelancing for UK, European and US TV channels, corporations, universities, brands, theatres, movies, dramas, concerts – all the genres. Now I am a filmmaker, curator and educator.

I'd like to tell teenagers that you know who you are going be and what you are going to do in your journey. It's hard to see when you're young but the clues are in your experiences. The things that you are drawn to on your journeys are right there behind and in front of you.

Follow the clues and the journey will lead you to your path, regardless of what other people say you should or shouldn't be able to do. Your passion for what you love is your drive to make that happen. Something you do as a passion and not for pay shows your commitment. You may not start off by getting paid but eventually you will become an expert and the go-to person for that particular thing, and then money will come to fund the passion.

Then you realise that this is not just a job; it's your practice, your wellbeing, meditation, challenge, your thrill and adventure. Every risk is worth it for a positive cause!

Winstan Whitter, award-winning director,
cinematographer and film editor

Your Recipe for Burnout

We've said a bit about school and why we think it can cause problems for lots of people. We've also explained how people can go into burnout and what it is. If you're in a really stressful situation for a long period of time, you can stop being able to get yourself back in the Zone – and that's when you start to get burnt out. Your body says No More. It's your natural cut-out mechanism, like a fuse going in a plug or your batteries running out.

School is one of the most stressful things for many teenagers. Not only does school go on for a really long time, but also people often think it is so important that they have no way out. They know they hate it and they feel trapped. This is a recipe for burnout. Basically, you are highly stressed but you feel you can't leave and it goes on and on – and that's when you start being at risk of burnout.

High stress + Feeling trapped + Going on for years = Burnout likely

Exercise: Your Burnout Recipe

Think about your own situation. What are the ingredients that have made life and school stressful for you?

Some of the common ingredients young people tell us about include:

Bullying

Strict teacher

Too much homework

Everything too noisy/light/smelly

Boring lessons

Not allowed to go on school trip

Horrible food/not allowed to eat food I like

Feeling ashamed about finding work difficult

Teacher saying I wasn't trying

Getting into trouble for things

Nowhere to go at lunch time

P.E. and swimming

Exam pressure

Worrying about what will happen if you fail

Arguments with friends

Social media pressure

Feeling isolated

Detentions

No one seeming to care if I was there or not

Arguments with parents

Family problems

Lack of money

If you want to, you could draw your own recipe sheet listing all the ingredients that make your experiences so difficult.

A Quick Recap

People are at high risk of burnout when they spend all their time doing things they don't enjoy and when they feel they have no other options. This makes them feel trapped.

Lots of teenagers say they don't have time to do the things they enjoy anymore. School requirements take up most of their time and exploring new things doesn't feel possible in case you don't do well at them. Life becomes about doing things because you have to. All you can see are the years of drudgery stretching out ahead of you.

This is a recipe for burnout. You aren't doing things that really make you feel alive and you start to feel you are just going through the motions. In this chapter, you had a chance to think about all the different ingredients that have come together for you, and how they might have led you to burnout.

5

The Road to Recovery

Recovery

Okay, you're probably thinking, they've gone on enough about what burnout is and why school can cause burnout. I have some ideas about what happened and why my body has said STOP. But what do I do about it? Am I going to be like this for ever now? Will I spend the rest of my life feeling terrible and exhausted and enjoying nothing?

No. The good news is that you can recover from burnout and loads of people do.

The bad news (or maybe more good news, depending on your perspective) is that you can't just go back to life as it was before. Remember we said that burnout isn't a sign that there is anything wrong with you – it's a sign that something was wrong in your environment. It's a sign that your body is reacting to the world around you by saying, NO MORE OF THIS. If you recover and then go back to living your life just as you did before this happened, then you will just get burnt out again. You have to think about (and your parents need to think about) how to make sure things will be different this time around.

The other bad news is that recovery isn't automatic. It doesn't just happen. There are things that can stop you from recovering and can keep you stuck in those vicious traps we were talking about before.

This next section is about what you can do to recover – and what might stop you from doing so.

Wear and Tear

One way of thinking about recovering from burnout is to think of yourself as a motor vehicle. Yes, it seems stupid but bear with us for a moment. Vehicles are all different, and they're all suited to different terrains. Some cars are best in the city and fit neatly into parking spaces. Others have four-wheel drive and can go across rugged terrain – even through water and sand.

As a motor vehicle drives around, it suffers wear and tear. The tyres become worn or the brakes start to squeak. We have to look after our cars or they become less efficient. We fill them up with fuel or charge them, if they are electric; we clean the windscreen and change the oil. All of these things help them to keep running smoothly.

Motor vehicles are equipped with shock absorbers to prevent us from feeling all the bumps on the road. But if they go over too many bumps, the shock absorbers stop working well. We begin to feel the bumps more.

If a vehicle is not well suited to the terrain, wear and tear happens more quickly and is more damaging. If you drive a Mini off-road in the forest, you won't be very comfortable and you'll soon start damaging it. You might even get completely stuck and be unable to get the car out of a hole. You could end up being dragged home behind a pick-up truck. A Land Rover, by contrast, might be fine driving through the forest, but it isn't as well suited to town because it's too big to fit into parking spaces and it is not fuel-efficient.

When your vehicle is on a road that suits you and you're driving fine, then you're in the Zone. You can move forwards in the direction you want to go. You can manage obstacles or unexpected hazards and stay on the road. When things really start going wrong, you move out of the Zone; you are stuck off-road in the wrong vehicle and you're unsure how to get back.

This is a metaphor. (Or is it perhaps a simile? This is one of those questions that seemed very important at school and now doesn't feel so important at all.) A metaphor is when you use an object (a motor vehicle, for example) to represent something else (a person, in this case). We are not saying you are really a vehicle. Thinking about yourself in this way can help you understand why some people get burnt out – and what you can do to help yourself recover.

People are Different

Each person is different, and we all react differently to the world around us. Well, doh!, you're probably thinking. Tell me something I don't know! But it's actually really important. We don't all enjoy the same things. Some people love loud busy places, while others prefer the quiet of the countryside. Some people enjoy playing video games in their spare time, while others do puzzles, go running or read a book. Some people like relaxing on a beach; others find the sun and the sand irritating and gritty and prefer to lie on the sofa at home. Some people even like doing things like sky-diving for fun – one of Naomi's nightmares.

There's nothing right or wrong with any of these things. It isn't better to like the beach or prefer the woods. One of these preferences isn't better than the others – it's just how people are.

Creating the World Around Us

Because we are all different, we make choices that help us shape the world around us to suit ourselves as best we can. We choose to wear comfortable rather than scratchy clothes. When we are adults, we choose where to live, the jobs that suit us and the people we spend our time with. We create our own world.

When our world is flexible and we have lots of choices, we can change things around us to suit ourselves. Both Naomi and Eliza work for themselves rather than having a boss. This means we can work the hours we like and choose the work we do or don't do. Other people prefer the routine of a full-time job, and the security of knowing they will get paid the same each week. Some people choose to work with their hands, while others do a lot of thinking and writing. In some jobs, you will spend every day surrounded by other people. This would not suit those of us who prefer to be alone, listening to a podcast.

It isn't always straightforward to find what works for you. Sometimes people make choices and then discover those choices didn't make them happy. Naomi went to university to study medicine and then discovered she really wasn't that interested in the finer details of how bodies worked nor of how drugs could change that. She did medicine for two years but then the chance came to study psychology for a year. She was amazed to discover just how much more interesting it was for her. She dropped out of medicine and became a psychologist instead.

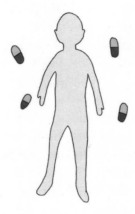

It wasn't easy dropping out, even though she knew she preferred psychology. She wondered if she was making a mistake and lots of people asked her if she was sure or whether it wouldn't be better to finish medicine first and qualify to be a doctor 'just in case'. She wasn't 100% sure, but she thought she had to give it a go.

There is often no way of knowing whether a choice is the right one or not except to try it out. Naomi has been learning about psychology for over twenty years now and she still finds it fascinating. She feels really lucky to have had the chance to study psychology, as she thinks she could have become an unhappy doctor. She didn't find medicine as interesting as psychology.

But there was no way to know that when she was choosing to study medicine. She thought it was the right thing at the time. For other people she studied with, medicine was the right choice and they have gone on to be happy and fulfilled doctors. Choices that are right for one person can be wrong for another. This is one reason why having choices is so important.

Exercise: What's Your Motor Vehicle Like?

If you were to imagine yourself as a motor vehicle, what would it be like? Are you tough and built for rough country, or more of a city car? Of course, you don't have to restrict yourself to a real car – what type of vehicle would you like to be? A flying boat? An underwater helicopter? An amphibious multi-tasker? You could draw it if that's your thing, or just write a description. You could even sew it or model it if you wanted to. It doesn't matter what it looks like. No one is testing you on this.

What environment is your vehicle suited to? Is it good in the jungle, or better in the desert? Where does it really excel, and where does it start to fall apart?

When the World Around Us Isn't Right

When you're in an environment that doesn't work for you, it takes a toll on you. If you're a person who really needs lots of quiet but you're stuck in a noisy, busy environment, you might be able to tolerate it for a bit, but over time it will get you down. It's like your vehicle is on the wrong type of road and it's getting damaged. Your shock absorbers are wearing down.

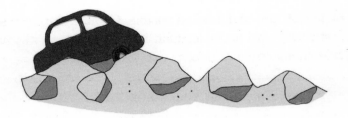

You might start to have headaches or stomach aches. You might start to feel irritable. Naomi had one job she really disliked. She had to sit in a busy open-plan office, right next to people having loud conversations on the phone. Ten people were jammed into the same room and the conversations were about distressing things. Naomi found it impossible to stop listening, even with noise-cancelling headphones.

After a few days, she started to feel prickly all over her skin. She found it hard to sleep. She had headaches even before she got to work. She quit that job after five weeks. She felt bad about letting people down but she couldn't see how the situation was going to improve. The environment made her feel physically ill. When she looked for a new job, she asked how many people she would have to share an office with. She never again took another job with an open-plan office. She hadn't actually known this would be a problem until she tried it out – and luckily for her, she could leave that job before it made her really sick.

When you are young, you have fewer choices than adults do. Your parents and/or other adults make decisions for you about where you will live, who you will live with, how you will be educated and, often, how you spend your time. This makes it harder for you to create an environment that works for you. You might be able to choose how your room is painted, who your friends are or how you spend your time after school and at weekends, but sometimes you can't even make those decisions. Lots of things are decided for you. This can be particularly hard if you are someone who likes things to be a certain way.

Then there's school. School is a place with very few choices. It's normal for young people to spend years and years in school with no choices about what they do every day. One of the weirdest things about school is that the people who get to make the most choices there are the youngest ones. Nursery and reception children can usually choose what they do from the activities on offer but, by the time you are thirteen or fourteen, you have no choices at all. You might not even be able to go to the toilet or get a drink of water when you want to. At nursery school, if a child goes to the toilet by themselves, everyone is pleased and tells them how grown up they are. Sometimes, it can seem as if your only choices at school are between doing what you are told and conforming, or getting into trouble. That's not much of a choice.

Some teenagers tell us they feel the person they are doesn't really matter at school. It doesn't matter if you are someone who loves art, you've still got to do all the other subjects. Your passion could even be something that never gets covered at school at all – like psychology.

I remember enjoying lots of the learning and activities in primary school. I had friends and liked some of the teachers a lot but I had lots of misunderstandings with friends and teachers too. I seemed to be involved in a lot of 'incidents', where I would feel upset or unfairly treated by teachers or my friends. These affected me a lot and left me feeling exhausted and low. I had lots of days off with illness, either real or pretend.

This carried on to secondary school, but now I found the environment overwhelming. The size, the smell and the demands of work were too much most of the time. Luckily, I had some close friendships and home, which offset the misery of being picked on and feeling bored or frustrated with the school work.

I think I appeared sociable and was in the top sets but, looking back, the number of illnesses and meltdowns I had at home were clear indicators of how much I was struggling to cope.

It took a lot of trying things out to get where I am; I had many different college placements that I failed to finish. I loved art college but self-sabotaged it when it became too much. The tutors wanted me to apply to the really good art colleges to do a degree, so I stopped going.

I moved from London to Brighton in my late teens and met lots of like-minded people and I did odd jobs, such as working in video shops, florists and an art-house cinema. I loved this last job and it didn't exhaust or bore me.

I was always drawing and writing, selling prints and then, when I met my ex-husband, we set up a design business where I designed wallpapers and he made furniture. It got a lot of media interest at the time but I didn't feel that passionate about it.

Doing what I do now has the emotional investment I need to feel the drive to do it. I am the most motivated I have ever felt now.

I earn my own money and have begun to travel. I am proud to say it has taken a long time to get here.

I would like to tell teenagers to take your time. You shouldn't have to know what you want to be yet. Try things out, have a go. If you don't like something, then try something else. It is as important to know what you do like as what you don't like.

Find good, true, honest friendships with those who won't judge you and who you'll be happy to sit in pyjamas with and put the world to rights. This is your life and it can look any way you want it to.

*Eliza Fricker (*Missing the Mark*),*
author and illustrator

Eliza remembers just wanting to draw at school, but she had to spend her time doing all the other subjects, too, because there was no other option. She didn't pass her exams in Mathematics and Science and she didn't go on to university – but she is still drawing. Now, she makes her living from it and has published several illustrated books, including this one.

Hostile Terrain

Okay, back to our motor vehicle metaphor. If you are the car, the world around you is the road or terrain. When you have enough choices and enough time to get to know yourself and what works for you, you can find a place in the world that works for you.

You can find a road on which your vehicle runs smoothly without too much strain. But if you are forced to travel on a road that isn't right for your vehicle, then not only will you start to feel the strain, you will also never have a chance to discover what the right road might look like.

You can't really get to know yourself if you are just concentrating on surviving in a challenging environment. When Naomi was putting all her energy into studying medicine, she couldn't find out that what really interested her was psychology. Medicine took up all her time and mental space. It wasn't until she stopped studying it that she could start to discover psychology.

School can be like that for lots of young people. It takes up so much of their time and energy just getting through each day that they haven't got anything left to discover what they really enjoy. It can feel like it doesn't really matter what they enjoy because – like Eliza – they aren't allowed to do what they want anyway.

Being in an environment where you have very few choices, which doesn't suit you and your unique characteristics and you can't leave or stop going for years on end, makes burnout likely. It's like a little Mini car being driven through the African savannah, over tree trunks and dried-up riverbeds, day after day with no chance of finding a smooth tarmacked road. The car will start to develop problems. Maybe the tyres will wear out, or the brakes will start to fail. If you keep on driving despite the problems, they will become more serious. Eventually, the car will stop. Something will break and it won't be able to carry on.

A Quick Recap

This chapter has been about differences, and how different people thrive in different environments. When you were younger, you might have watched animated films where the characters sang songs telling you to 'Be just who you are' as they flew around. Now you're a teenager, however, it can feel as if who you are is only valued when you do what everyone else wants you to do.

Most of us know that we are all different, but sometimes we don't really think about what this actually means. What works for one person might not work at all for someone else, even the things that everyone is supposed to do.

We've used the metaphor of a vehicle as an example. If you try driving a Mini through the jungle, you will soon run into problems. This doesn't mean there's anything fundamentally wrong with the Mini. (At least, there wasn't until it was driven through the jungle and sank into a swamp.) It just means that Minis are not well suited to jungle driving; they're better for getting around town and sneaking into small parking spaces. A Jeep would be better in the jungle, but not so practical in town.

When we can make choices, most of us change our environment to suit ourselves. When we have few choices in life, this can be much harder to do.

6

Breakdown

The Four Stages of Recovery

We've talked about how burnout happens, and maybe you have some ideas now as to why it might have happened to you. We've used the metaphor of a vehicle needing to suit the terrain it's travelling through – different vehicles are suited to different terrains. Things in your life, like your school, are a particular terrain and it might not be well suited to you; perhaps it is too pressured for you. When there's a mismatch between you and your environment, you can be at risk of burnout. Just living your life can take a toll on you and push you out of the Zone. It doesn't have to be a big thing that happens. Lots of little things all add up.

What happens next, then? How do people recover from burnout? Research shows that there are four main stages people go through when recovering. The stage you are at makes a difference to what might help. As you read, you'll probably recognise yourself and where you are.

Stage 1: Breakdown

That's when you reach burnout. The day when you just can't do it anymore. When you can't get out of bed, or you just can't make yourself put on your school uniform. Or, for some young people, it happens when something goes wrong at school and that is the last straw.

SCHOOL

This stage of recovery is the crisis stage. It's as if your vehicle has just been in an accident and you are standing by the side of the road, upset and not really sure what has happened to you. Your emotions will be all over the place and you could feel upset without knowing why. Perhaps you feel physically ill and sleep for ages. It's possible everything feels very unstable and lots of things are changing really quickly. Suddenly, you might stop going to school after months and years of being unhappy, for example.

For Oliver, it happened when a teacher at school told him to get a haircut. He'd been unhappy at school for a long time and he'd been growing his hair. It was long and dark and he liked it. When the science teacher told him he looked scruffy and he should go to the barber, Oliver was pushed beyond what he could stand. He walked out of school and didn't go back. No one could understand why; it was just a haircut! When his parents explained, the school couldn't see the problem. But for Oliver, it was the final straw.

Little Things Push You Over the Edge

Burnout doesn't happen overnight but sometimes it can seem like it does. It happens as a result of the accumulation of so many tiny things, all of which are like tiny pinpricks. You hardly notice the first ones, but as time goes on it becomes harder and harder to keep going. It's like your vehicle is taking lots of small hits – you start to notice little bits of rust and chips out of the windscreen, while little problems with the engine start to occur. It's manageable – until it's not anymore. The fan belt goes and the car is off the road.

Because it can seem like a tiny thing that pushes you into burnout, it's hard for others to understand why you can't carry on. Sometimes, something you have done hundreds of times before suddenly becomes too much. It was like that for Emma. She found school intensely stressful but she did everything she was meant to do. People thought of her as a studious person and she always did her homework on time. Then one day, the class was assigned a particularly heavy load of homework. Mathematics, reading for English and a chapter in the Geography textbook. Emma also had school orchestra that day and so she didn't get home until nearly 6 p.m. She got home, got out her books and she couldn't do it. She just couldn't. She heard a strange buzzing in her head and she found it hard to focus.

Her parents didn't understand. Emma had always been able to do her homework before and there wasn't anything different about today. Emma couldn't understand it either. But she just couldn't carry on. It felt like something had broken inside. She went to school the next day but she couldn't concentrate at all. She felt dizzy. She went to the school nurse and was sent home. Then she found that she just couldn't go back the next day and that even leaving her room started to feel impossible. She felt like she had a brick wall behind her eyes, but no one seemed to understand what that was like. She wasn't sure what had happened but it felt like she was at the point of no return. Something had snapped inside her. She could do nothing except lie in bed. Even listening to a podcast gave her a headache.

When you're in the Breakdown phase of burnout, it can be pretty scary. You might not know what is going on and other people will probably think you must be physically ill. You might get taken to the doctor. You feel like you can't go on anymore, but you look the same as usual from the outside. No one understands that your body has reached its limit and it's not a choice you have control over.

Often, what happens at this stage is that people try to guilt-trip you or pressure you into going back to school or returning to your previous life. This makes everything worse. You know it's not good and you don't want to feel like this, but you can't carry on. Other people might say you've decided to do this, but to you it doesn't feel like a choice. It's not a choice. Your body is saying No More.

Unhelpful Things People Say

People often say very unhelpful things at this point. Adults try to persuade you to go back to life as it was, as if all that is needed is a bit more pressure and you'll stop feeling this way. These unhelpful things are usually disguised as 'helpful', but all they do is pile on the pressure.

The table you see below gives some examples You could also add your own unhelpful 'helpful' things people have said to you. You could even treat it like a *Bingo* board and tick off all the ones you've heard.

	You're letting yourself down		You'll get behind	
		You will never catch up		
	If you don't pass your GCSEs you'll end up under a bridge			You've been doing so well this year, don't stop now!
What a shame to mess up your attendance record		If you don't come back to school your parents could go to prison		

You are probably feeling pressured from many angles. School, your parents and yourself.

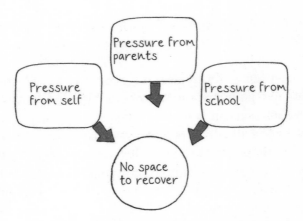

It all adds up to having no space at all to recover. Remember, we said it is possible not to recover from burnout? Well, this is one way to prevent recovery. Pressure. Pressure will mean you don't have the space to relax, and you need to relax before you can start finding your way back to the Zone.

The essential truth here is this.

You can't use pressure and anxiety to help you feel less pressured and anxious.

Well, doh.

What do I do instead?

The opposite of pressure is time and space to breathe.

To get this space, you need people to stop pressuring you – and to stop pressuring yourself. You need time to recover and people to talk to who understand. These people could be your parents or other relatives, but they might not be. Sometimes, talking to parents can feel stressful, not because they want to stress you out but because they care so much. Sometimes that love can feel like pressure. Sometimes parents find it hard to stay calm and that isn't helpful either.

There is a guide for parents at the end of this book that they could read if you are finding it hard to talk to them.

You could also ask them to help you find another adult to talk to – perhaps a counsellor or psychologist, but it could also be a relative or a good friend. Some people have found tutors or music teachers with whom they feel comfortable and able to be themselves.

We would not recommend finding people by yourself over the internet or talking about how you feel on Discord servers and WhatsApp groups. It is very hard to tell whom you are talking to over the internet, and the things you say could be used in ways you had not anticipated. Anything you say can be screenshot and shared around and you lose control of your words.

Be wary of people you haven't met who tell you they understand you better than your parents do. They do not really know you, even if they say they do. They do not have your best interests at heart – they can't do, because they do not know you.

At this stage, you are in the emergency stage of recovery. It's as if you've had an accident and you're still injured. You need good food, comfort and nice things to do that aren't demanding. This is the time to watch a box set with your dad or play a video game you've played loads of times before and know well. Or, you could read a book or listen to an audiobook again that you used to love. Don't worry if you don't enjoy those things in the way you usually do. This is normal in this stage of burnout. You will almost certainly feel like you don't want to do anything because it won't be enjoyable – try doing some of them anyway.

It's also a time to surround yourself with positive things to give yourself the best chance of recovery. Sometimes, people find communities online that are very negative about the world. If you're feeling negative yourself, this can feel really good at first; you've found a group of people who seem to understand you. What a relief! They might even say they know what you're going through and they have the solution. Many of these communities are identity-focused – they will tell you that if you identify in the same way as they do, you'll feel happier and you'll belong with them. They may tell you that feeling the way you do means you definitely have a particular identity. But as you start to recover, these communities can bring you down and stop you from being able to move forwards.

Lifting the Pressure

Parents	Get them to read the parents' guide at the end of this book.
	Ask them to stop pressuring you while you recover. Tell them what you find pressuring.
	If you find it hard to talk to them, ask them to find someone else you could talk to.
	See if there are any low-pressure things you could do with your parents – maybe playing a game together or cooking.

	Ask your parents not to ask you pressuring questions like, 'Are you going back to school today?' or 'Have you thought about which courses to take?' They will not help at this stage and could make things worse.
School	Read stories about people who have succeeded outside school (there are some examples in this book).
	Ask your parents not to pass on messages from school if you find them pressuring.
	Decide for yourself whether it helps to have contact with people you knew from school – you can take a break. You can say that you have been advised to do this by a psychologist (Naomi!) if you don't know how to tell people you need a break.
Self	Ask yourself what helps you feel better and worse and do more of the things that help you feel better (or just not worse).
	Take yourself out of negative communities or groups.
	Consider taking a social-media break.
	Spend time with people with whom you feel comfortable.
	Try the Container exercise opposite.
	Find some physical exercise you can do easily and do it every day. Even if you feel exhausted and can only do two minutes. Some consoles have exercise games, or there are YouTube videos you can use if it is too much to leave the house.

Pressurising Yourself

Reducing the pressure you feel from your own thoughts and feelings is tough. You really can't get away from pressure when it's inside your own head. However, you can learn ways to manage this pressure, but it takes practice.

Our brains naturally fall into thinking in the same ways – it's as if they become automated or get stuck in a rut. If you've been putting pressure on yourself for a long time, you can't just stop overnight. You have to deliberately try to retrain your thinking to give yourself a break. The Container exercise is one way to do this.

Exercise: The Container

Many people find themselves consumed with worries about the future or about the past. There is nothing they can do about the future or the past, and so the worries just go round and round. This makes them feel very pressured. They can ruin the present, while not helping you to change anything.

This is an imagery exercise that some people find useful. It might be hard at first but it often gets easier with practice. Imagery just means that it's about you creating things in your imagination. Some people find this easy to do, while others find it hard. If you find it hard, you can find real pictures or draw things rather than imagining them.

We are going to create an imaginary container. You can decide for yourself what this container is like. It can be just in your head or real. If you want to, you can draw or model it, or find a photo online.

Some of the teenagers we know have chosen a safe, a swimming-pool locker, or a vault in a bank. One person chose a goblet with a lid.

Once you have created your container, you imagine putting the thoughts and feelings that are getting you down into that container.

It will keep them safe until you need them. You aren't trying to make them disappear, you are placing them somewhere for safekeeping.

Some people imagine pulling their thoughts out of their head using a wand or other device. Others imagine writing their thoughts down on paper and putting them into the container. Or throwing the thoughts into the container like pebbles.

If you are someone who finds imagining things hard, you can write down your thoughts on paper and actually put them into a container. We know someone who has a special lidded bowl in the corner of their room where they put their thoughts for safekeeping.

It's up to you how to go about doing this.

When the worrying thoughts are in the container, shut the container tight. The thoughts are safe inside. Now you can imagine putting that container somewhere. You could leave it with someone you trust, or you could hide it somewhere. Some people like to imagine batting the container out into the atmosphere to orbit the Earth until they need it.

Again, you could either imagine this or you could draw it or write about it. Some people find it very hard to just imagine things and prefer it when they can create something in the real world.

Now that the container is safe, you can focus your thoughts on doing something you enjoy. Active things work really well. Naomi usually imagines herself skiing or juggling, even though she isn't any good at either skiing or juggling. She imagines how she thinks it would feel to be good at those things, how great it would feel to be whooshing through the snow or catching the juggling balls. She imagines how it would feel in her body, how the snow would smell and how it would feel to be among the trees. If you find your thoughts going back to the worries in the container, just bring yourself back to the thing you enjoy.

If you find imagining things hard, then you could find something in real life. You could use a short video or piece of music to play to yourself.

One young person Naomi worked with used a piece of music they played in an orchestra. They found a YouTube video of it being played and would put it on and immerse themselves in the music. You could also dance or bounce to the music if that helps you.

Focus on how this feels in your body when you do something you enjoy. If any negative thoughts pop up, just put them back in that container.

You can do this exercise any time you find that your brain is getting caught up in worries and pressure. Don't worry if it doesn't seem to help at first, it really will get easier as you do it more.

Container Exercise Summary

1. Create a container (imaginary or use creativity).
2. Put your worrying thoughts into the container for safe-keeping. You can either imagine them, or write them down and actually put them in a container.
3. Hide the container somewhere secure (either imaginary or real). Your thoughts and feelings are safe in the container.
4. Bring your thoughts to something you enjoy (or use a video or piece of music) and notice how this feels in your body and brain. If your thoughts go to the worries, gently bring them back to the activity you enjoy.

There is No Quick Fix

When you are feeling utterly terrible and you don't really understand why, it's tempting to look for answers that solve everything. It would be amazing if there was one thing you could change that will make everything else better.

You may come across people (often on the internet but also in real life and in books) who will tell you that they know why you are feeling the way you do, and that if you do what they say, identify in the way they do, buy their course or join in their community, everything in your life will improve. Sometimes, people will say that you need a particular diagnosis, or you should take medication or identify in a certain way, and then everything will improve. Influencers post videos of themselves on YouTube and TikTok, saying how much better their life is since they realised that the problem was . . . (fill in many different answers here). They'll tell you the problem is that no one else understands you, because you are different, and that the world doesn't understand people like you. They may tell you that your parents have no idea who you really are, and that you can't trust them to be on your side.

These communities and influencers can appear to be the hope at the end of the tunnel. It can be such a relief to think that you've got the answer now, you understand why everything went wrong and you can fix it. It can be great to have a sense of belonging, that there are other people like you, and to think that there is a simple reason for your problems.

However, there's a downside. Influencers do not really care about or know you. They care about getting Likes and Shares. The more people see their videos, the more money they make. That means they are going to say things they know attract an audience and keep them coming back.

Unfortunately, there are lots of unhappy teenagers who are trying to understand why they are so unhappy, and so there are thousands of influencers producing videos suggesting that they have the answer (and they will tell you that other people just don't get it, so you have to keep coming back to their content).

This isn't to say that online communities can't be great – they can be. But they can also influence our thinking in ways we're not necessarily aware of – just like advertising does. Their motivation isn't necessarily to help you. It's to convince you that you need their content and to keep coming back for it. Sometimes, the things they say to get you to do this can actually make things worse in the long term. They can be a trap, stopping you from starting to feel better.

Things to Look Out For

Red Flag	Reality
People suggesting there is a simple solution to your problems and if you just do X, everything will get better.	They don't know you and they don't know your problems. Life is complicated.
People saying that you can't trust your parents, that they don't know anything about what it's like to be a young person today.	They don't know your parents and what they know, and they don't know whether your parents are trustworthy or not.
People saying you need to find out what your True (or Authentic) Self is before you will be happy.	Discovering who you are is the work of a lifetime. Who you are will change at various times, depending on your experiences. You don't have to know everything about yourself when you are a teenager (or an adult, for that matter).

Saying that if people disagree with you or question you, they are hating on you or haters.	Disagreeing with someone is not the same as hating them. Questioning people is what others do when they want to better understand.
People implying that only they understand you, no one else can really understand you.	They don't know you and they don't know about other people in your life.
People saying when they started taking X (or identifying as X) they became so much happier overnight and their life was transformed.	There are many things that make people feel better in the short term but which in the longer term make things worse. This is the case for drinking, self-harm and taking many illegal drugs. Most change that lasts happens slowly over time.
Strict, unspoken rules about what can be said and done. Questions that cannot be asked or you'll get blocked or kicked out of servers.	These are signs that this is a controlling and possibly abusive community. It should always be okay to ask questions or disagree.
There's a clear 'in group' and 'out group'. People talk about those outside the group in a derogatory way. People who were previously in the 'in group' do something and then are publicly shamed and kicked out, and everyone considers them to be a bad person from then on.	This group is using fear of shaming to control its members. This means that people will not feel able to speak truthfully or be open, even if they say that they are.
People taking screenshots from private conversations or groups and posting them in other groups or in public.	This breaks the trust between members of a private conversation or group. It can create a lot of drama and will mean that people do not feel safe to say what they think for fear that it will be shared elsewhere.
People posting videos of themselves with scars, injecting drugs or hurting themselves, or videos of how much weight they have lost. People posting videos of themselves with symptoms of severe mental health problems.	These videos get a lot of attention and that is why they are there. They can be fascinating but they are primarily there to get your attention and to monetise it. You can never know how real any of it is.

If you are in online communities where you feel pressured to be a certain way, these will not be good for your mental health. You might not even notice the pressure, because it is the nature of control that it is undercover. People who appear to be lovely and accepting can also be controlling. One clue is if people are nice to you, but you've seen that when people disagree with them they'll block them and kick them out. Think about the people you hang out with online. Could you disagree with them? Would they stay friends with you if you said you didn't think something they were doing was right? Or would they block you immediately?

However you feel about your online world, I'd recommend taking a break from social media and internet communities while you are in the early stages of burnout recovery. You need mental and emotional space to recover, and sometimes you can only see things clearly once you've been away from them for a while. You can always go back. They will still be there.

A Quick Recap

Lots of people get to a point where they just can't go on anymore and sometimes this happens quite quickly. Something goes wrong one day and it's the final straw. You just can't keep going. We call this the Breakdown stage.

When this happens, it's confusing for everyone and there can be lots of pressure on you to get back to 'normal' as soon as possible. This won't help. The thing that is most important in the Breakdown stage is that you get some time and space to recover, and you can't do that if there is pressure on you. Even if that pressure is coming from you. You can't use pressure and anxiety to make yourself feel less pressured and anxious.

Lots of things can make you feel pressured, including school, your parents and things online. This chapter has some suggestions of ways you can lift that pressure off to give yourself some space to recover.

7

Repair

Stage 2: Repair

Once the crisis is over, everything settles down a bit. It's not such a shock anymore. You might have stopped going to school or you might be doing much less than you were, and while everyone was not okay with that at first, now they are more used to the idea.

This stage of recovery is like being at the mechanics. Your vehicle is off the road and has been moved to a safe place. The intense crisis stage is over. Now you need repairs. You need new oil, your engine tuned up, repairs to your shock absorbers and brakes and a lot of TLC. It's not the time to worry about the future. It's the time to focus on looking after yourself now.

How to Not Get Better

The quickest way to stop your recovery, in our experience, is if you or the people around you are looking out for any sign that you might be ready to go back to your old life. Sometimes people will say unhelpful things like, 'If you're well enough to go to the shops, you're well enough to go to school.'

This sort of comment can actively stop you recovering, because it means you can't do anything at all in case people say you must go back to your old life immediately.

In order to recover from burnout, you need to regain your ability to get yourself back into the Zone. You need to start to connect with the parts of yourself you used to have when you were in the Zone. It's remembering how you used to be before you got stuck in this state of chronic stress.

All the things from the previous chapter still apply. Pressure will not help. Spending lots of time in online communities is unlikely to help. You need some real-life contact with people who get you, and some time to do things you enjoy.

Remember Your Passions

Now is the time to reconnect with your previous passions and let yourself go down some rabbit holes. What are the things you used to find interesting and how can you do more of those things? Things you do with your hands and body can be particularly helpful. Maybe you used to love making slime when you were younger and you could do that again. Kinetic sand or silly putty can be lots of fun. Cooking is often great – with or without a recipe – and so is swimming, singing or climbing.

You might be judging my suggestions as you read this. You might be thinking that you've grown out of these things and they are childish. You might be thinking, But I need to get back to school and exams. How is slime-making going to help me with that? Or maybe other people are saying these sorts of things to you.

The reason we are suggesting things like these is that they are often activities where people do not feel pressured. They are the things people do when they are in their Zone, and they help keep you in the Zone. It's often comforting to go back to things you used to enjoy. Naomi used to read the same books over and over when she was a teenager. She still remembers some of the words now. There were no surprises and no stress. People would tell her she should be reading new books and this was even written in her school report, but they didn't understand why she was reading. It wasn't to learn new things or challenge herself. It helped her feel safe. Familiarity is really comforting when things are tough.

It's really unlikely that you will feel pressure to make slime to an A* standard, or that people are assessing how you play with kinetic sand. These activities are things you do just because you enjoy them – and are the sort of things you need to do at this stage.

There may be other things that work for you – some people have very strong passions and they find that following those passions and learning about them helps them start to feel alive again. Jake was someone like that.

Jake's Story

Jake was fifteen and had had a really bad time at school. He had frequent stomach aches and at his primary school they said he was malingering (meaning, they thought he was making it up to get out of school). He went to a specialist secondary school where some of the other kids got very angry and threw furniture and broke windows. He started to be scared every day. One day he went to school and the boy he sat next to spat at him. That was enough for Jake. He walked out and did not go back.

Jake very quickly found that he was tired all the time and felt hopeless about the future. His body felt heavy. He didn't want to leave the house. Whenever he felt a tiny bit better, his parents said maybe he could go back to school the next day and he felt worse again. He was stuck.

When Naomi met Jake, he was in the Breakdown stage and he needed everyone to back off. Jake's parents agreed to stop talking about returning to school and to give Jake some space.

Jake has a strong interest in escapology, and he found it comforting to take locks apart and put them back together again. He started doing that several times a day. Over time, he started to look up videos on how to make his own locks. His parents helped him get materials and he also made videos of his locks. He started to feel a bit less tired when he was doing that and even enjoyed life for a few minutes – but the moment anyone suggested he might return to school or do something else, he felt terrible again.

Over time, Jake's interest in escapology grew and he started designing his own escape rooms for his family and friends. He wanted to make online escape rooms so he started learning some coding in order to do so. Little by little, Jake started to feel life was worth living again.

Exercise: Doing More of What You Enjoy

Spend a bit of time thinking about the things that really interest you. What do you love hearing about/reading/watching? You might find that as you start to think about this you are self-censoring, thinking, Well, that's a waste of time. Maybe you've been told your interests aren't worthwhile.

This is the time to allow yourself to think about what you enjoy and what makes you feel alive, even if others think it's not worth the time. Other teenagers tell me they are interested in guitar, drumming, programming, chess, poker, football, skateboarding, fashion, anime, graphic novels, bouldering, animal care, or beauty and makeup.

When you've identified some things you enjoy, ask yourself two questions.

1) Do I get a chance to do this thing regularly?
2) If not, how could I make time for it in my life?

Make yourself a plan. What would be one small step towards making more time to do the things that you enjoy?

Sleep

In the early stages of burnout, it's common for your sleep to be all over the place. You might find that you can't sleep at night, or you can't stop sleeping. You might sleep and sleep and never feel refreshed, or you might never sleep, even though you are so tired you can hardly move. You might have what is called day–night reversal – you are awake all night and asleep all day. You might even be pleased about this because it means that you never have to see annoying people and you definitely can't go back to school, because you are asleep all day.

Sleep is a strange thing. We can't just sleep whenever we want to. (At least, Eliza and Naomi can't; you might be different.) Our body needs a rhythm in order to sleep well – there is a gland in our body that releases hormones at night that make us sleepy, and then different hormones in the morning to wake us up.

Sleep changes during puberty. When you start to go through puberty, it's common for people who used to wake up early every day to suddenly want to sleep in until midday and stay up late at night. This doesn't mean that you are lazy (even though sometimes unhelpful adults say that). It means that your hormonal balance has changed and the hormone that wakes you up in the mornings is now released later.

There's nothing wrong with sleeping late in the mornings and it's natural for most teenagers. However, what can sometimes happen is that you stay up later and later at night, perhaps because you are playing online with people in another country, and then you sleep later and later in the day. Sometimes, people sleep all day and then are awake all night. Or they only wake up at 4 or 5 p.m.

This does cause problems, because your body needs enough exposure to daylight in order to set your sleep rhythm. We know this sounds strange, but humans are animals. We are very responsive to our environment and the world around us, and we need to see daylight in order for our biological (called circadian) rhythms to work properly. When it is dark, our body is more likely to produce the hormones that help us to sleep. Sleeping all day and being up all night will mean that your sleep is not of good quality, which can keep you feeling fatigued and exhausted, even though you are sleeping for the same number of hours. Research with shift workers shows that when they have to sleep during the day and stay awake at night it has a long-term effect on their health. This sleep pattern also stops you from doing things you might enjoy, because they happen during the day and you are asleep.

You may be thinking, But I can't change when I go to sleep. I'm not tired any earlier. Because our sleep is controlled by our hormonal rhythm, changing when you sleep is not as simple as just going to bed earlier. If you've ever been jet-lagged, you know this already. Your body can still think it's in a different time zone, even when you have flown across the Atlantic. This can mean you are ready for bed at 3 p.m. – or not ready until 3 a.m.

Changing your sleep pattern is a gradual thing. Here are some ideas on how to do it that might help.

Problem	Strategy
Sleeping all day	Set an alarm clock slightly earlier each day. One day, get up at 4 p.m. Do this for a few days to get used to it. Then, set the alarm for 3.30 p.m. Give yourself time to get used to this and then move it to 3 p.m. (and so on).
Not tired at night	Make sure you are getting some exposure to daylight during the day. Go out, even if just for a short time. Increase how much you are doing during the day and how much you move your body.
Tired all the time but not able to sleep	Try to increase the amount of exercise you do during the day, even if you feel totally exhausted. Ideally, go out and get exercise in the daylight. It doesn't necessarily have to be playing sports. Walking is fine.
Takes ages to get to sleep	Plan a wind-down period in the evenings. Don't play your favourite games or read the most interesting books in the evening. Have some time in the evenings when you aren't looking at a screen, as this can stop you sleeping. Drink camomile tea and have a bath before you go to bed if that helps you feel sleepy.
Thoughts start going round and round when I go to bed	Find a calming audio book or podcast to listen to in bed. Find a reader with a voice you like but don't choose anything too exciting. Some people find meditation apps helpful, while others don't.
Tired at a different time every day	Try setting an alarm clock at a realistic time and start trying to get up at that time. Make sure you get outside and see some daylight when you wake up.

Sleep and rest don't help me feel refreshed	If you are feeling fatigued all the time even though you are sleeping for a long time every night, the problem might not be lack of sleep or rest. You might, instead, be lacking stimulation in your life. Even if you don't feel like it, try doing some things you used to enjoy, or find yourself a new game to play or book to read. Try getting out into the daylight and moving your body more each day.

Feeling Sad

Lots of people feel very sad at this stage in burnout recovery. It can take you by surprise because it might seem like the crisis is over now, and you should feel relieved that you aren't going to school anymore.

But instead, lots of kids say they feel very sad that they aren't having the life they thought they should be having – going to school, going out with friends, taking exams. They feel as if their future has been cancelled and a void has opened up. Even if you hated school and have been pushing yourselves through it for years, when you finally stop, it is a shock.

If this is you, it's natural to feel like this. Feelings come and go. It can help to talk to someone else, or some people find it helps to write music or poetry that expresses how they feel. Some people do art to help process their feelings. Eliza started drawing her cartoons to help her come to terms with her own experiences as the mother of a person for whom school didn't work, and then she started to draw pictures about her own experiences growing up. Naomi started writing about her difficulties with school in the 1980s and '90s when she was called a 'school refuser' or 'school-phobic'.

Out of the Garage

After a while, you might start to feel a bit differently. One day, you might notice that you are enjoying doing something again. You might make an elaborate cake for your sister's birthday and actually get excited about multiple colours of fondant icing.

Maybe you find yourself starting to feel a bit bored with staying at home all the time and start to wonder about taking a trip to the local shop or park. You notice that sometimes there are a few moments of feeling okay. You might start to feel interested in something again, or excited because a new game or series is coming out.

Part of you might feel scared of this feeling because you are worried that if you do get better, people will make you go back to school. This is where it is really important to talk to your parents and make sure you are all on the same page. Things need to change in the world around you for you to be able to keep going and keep yourself in the Zone. Recovery is not back to 'business as usual'. If that is what happens, you may well get burnt out again.

At this stage, it can be helpful to deliberately notice the little moments when things are going well. We call these Glimmers – moments when you feel good, when your body feels relaxed, or when you start to feel interested in something again.

Exercise: Glimmers

As you go about your day, see if you can notice little moments when you feel okay. Even a second or two is enough. Maybe it's the first mouthful of a chocolate cake or seeing your little brother playing in the water sprinkler. Maybe it's a moment of interest when you see your favourite author has a new book coming out or a second of excitement about seeing a new film.

Keep a note of these somehow. You can do it on your phone or on a piece of paper. You could draw little pictures or write down a reminder for yourself about these moments.

These little glimmers can pass very quickly if we don't take note of them, and we can forget that they were there at all. By noticing them and keeping a record, you are helping to retrain your brain to start noticing the good things again. You are also noticing the moments when you are reconnecting with yourself again.

Quick Recap

When the Breakdown stage passes, everything starts to feel a bit less confusing and more stable. You still feel terrible, but it's less of a crisis. This is when you might start to move into the Repair stage of recovery.

At this point, what is important is reconnecting with yourself and the things you care about. Those things might be things you liked when you were much younger, or they might be things other people told you are a 'waste of time'. What matters is how you feel about them and that you enjoy them, not what they are.

You may feel totally numb and like you don't care about anything anymore, in which case it's about looking for the tiny glimmers, the moments when things aren't quite so bad. It's really common in the Repair stage to feel very sad and to have trouble sleeping, and this doesn't mean there's anything wrong. It's part of the process.

8

Learning from the Journey

Stage 3: Learning from the Journey

When you are starting to feel a bit better and you are able to do things you enjoy without pressure, it's finally the time to look behind you and work out what went wrong.

Don't rush into this stage. Adults are often really keen to start thinking about how to get you back on the road, particularly if you have exams coming up. The Breakdown and Repair stages are essential, and they need to happen with as little pressure as possible. They can take months. Exams can be taken at any stage; there is no magic age for them. In the future, it really will not matter whether you took your exams when you were sixteen or eighteen or you found a way to move on in your life without exams. It will matter much more whether you had time to really recover from burnout. Recovery needs to happen now and it is the most important thing.

This is the stage of thinking about all the things that made your life so stressful, without judgement. Your old thought patterns were probably all about how your difficulties with school are your fault, and you should just try harder and stop complaining. They kept you going to school, but they also pushed you into burnout.

It's time for a reset.

Resetting Your Thought Patterns

It's not easy to reset the way you think and it doesn't just happen. It's another one of those things you need to practise doing deliberately. We outline below a process some people find helpful for this. Doing it with someone else can also help if you have an adult you trust.

The first stage is to notice the thoughts that automatically pop into your head when you start to think of your past experiences. Thoughts like, I'm a failure, or, It was all my fault. We call these 'automatic thoughts'.

Write them down.

Then, write down the things you have learnt from this book that do not fit with these automatic thoughts. Things like, School doesn't work for everyone, and, the way my body responds to chronic stress is not my fault, and, you can't reduce pressure by adding pressure.

Lastly, see if you can reframe those automatic thoughts so they are more realistic and kinder to yourself. For example, you might say to yourself, I'm someone who finds school extremely stressful, rather than, It was all my fault. Or you could say, I can succeed in many different ways, rather than, I'm a failure.

If you find this really hard, try writing down your list and then putting it away for a while. When you get it out again, pretend that a friend has come to you to ask for help with their thoughts. What alternatives would you suggest for them?

Automatic Thought	New Information	Alternative Thought
I am a failure	Not everyone can succeed at school. School is set up to be a competition.	I can succeed in different ways.
It's my fault I am burnt out.	Our bodies respond to chronic stress by saying, No More. That is not a choice.	It's not my fault this happened.
I will never amount to anything.	School is only one way to learn. Lots of people who don't do well at school go on to have great lives.	I will find a way to live an interesting life.
I am weak and silly to respond like this.	We all respond in different ways to our environments. This doesn't mean that some reactions are better than others.	I can build on my experiences and learn more about myself.

It's hard to remember alternative thoughts. You can write them down so you have them ready when the automatic thoughts pop up. Or you could do something creative with them, such as setting them to music or incorporating them into art work.

Friendships and Relationships

One of the things that often changes as you go through puberty is that relationships with other people your own age get more important. Lots of little kids don't have many friends and are fine with it. They are happy with their parents and family.

Then, as you get older, having friends matters more. Parts of your brain change as you become a teenager and this means you start to care more about what people around your own age think of you. It hurts when people leave you out or don't want to be friends with you. Those feelings can be really intense.

At school, it is particularly important to have a group of people to hang out with. Without them, you feel exposed and have no one to eat with at lunch and nowhere to go at break time. Sometimes, it's hard to tell who your real friends are and who you are with just because you need the cover. You might feel you can't be yourself with them because it's so important to fit in that you can't say what you really think or do what you like to do. Perhaps you felt pressurised to have a romantic or sexual relationship when you didn't actually want to, because everyone else seemed to expect it.

Sometimes, the people you believe are your friends might tell you to do things that get you into trouble. These people can have a lot of power over you because you don't want to be left on your own and so you do things you don't really want to do or that you know are wrong.

When you are burnt out and starting to recover, often part of the process is thinking about your friendships and realising that some of them are not really friendships at all. You might realise that you felt pressured to be part of a group, or to look like you have lots of friends, which means you have spent time with people who don't help you feel good about yourself.

When you are at school, lots of the people you meet might not have that much in common with you. You are just all together because you are the same age, and so you have to get on with each other. There isn't much choice about who is in your class, and you can get stuck with them for years on end. It can feel as if you'll never meet people you really connect with.

You might be happy not having friends your own age or only having online friends and, if so, that's fine. There are many different ways to be. However, if you want friends but haven't found any at school, then you might have to be more intentional about the process and create the opportunities for you to find new friends.

Lots of teenagers who do not find good friends at school meet like-minded people through doing things they enjoy. It's a more deliberate process than just being in the same school class as people. You might decide to join something, hoping to meet people you get along with. You might even set up a group (or ask your parents to help you set up a group) to do something you enjoy and ask a couple of people who you think might be interested. Those people won't necessarily be in the same school year as you, but they will share an interest with you.

> Teenagers we know have met friends through:
> Singing in a choir
> Bouldering
> Playing *Dungeons and Dragons*
> Board game café meet-ups
> Playing in a wind band or orchestra
> Climbing
> Art classes
> Scouts or Guides or Woodcraft Folk
> Online gaming
> Life-guarding lessons
> Outdoor activity groups
> Youth Clubs
> Skateboarding
> Windsurfing
> Football
> Teen yoga or meditation classes
> Teen sessions at the local gym

Perhaps you're at a time in your life when you really don't feel much of a connection with people your own age and you worry that you're missing out because other teenagers seem to be hanging out in big groups. There will always be lots of people who aren't in the big groups – you just don't notice them because they are elsewhere. There are many different ways to be and you might be someone who needs more alone time, or who prefers to have one or two good friends rather than lots of group friends. It's easy to feel that teenagers have to all be a certain way but that isn't true. There are many ways to be a teenager, just like there are many ways to be every other age.

Looking Behind You

Now's the moment to take a long, honest look at your life up to this point. What are the things that put you under stress? Try to think about them without judgement. Don't blame yourself. Right now, we're just collecting information about what is hard for you.

Sometimes, parents can be helpful at this stage. They might have noticed things you hadn't noticed – like the way that you were most stressed on Mondays because you knew you had PE first thing and you had nightmares about being last-picked for the teams in PE. They also might be ready to tell you stories from when you were younger about how you reacted to different things, which can be important clues about what you find stressful.

These are some common things teenagers tell us they find stressful. Some of them might apply to you and others won't. You'll probably have your own things that we haven't included.

Other people	Bullying. Arguments. Pressure to fit in or be a certain way. Feeling you have nothing in common with other people your age. Being surrounded by others all day.
Exams	Having to take lots of exams at the same time. Pressure to do well in exams. Repeated emphasis on exams and lots of practice exams.
Friendship drama	Friendship groups where someone is always arguing or calling other people toxic. People getting thrown out of friendship groups. Friends saying they won't be your friend if you don't behave in a particular way.
Rules	Rules that seem silly to you but which you have to keep anyway. Rules that do not take account of why you might be doing something. Strict consequences when you do not comply with the rules.

Teachers	Teachers saying things like, 'You shouldn't be struggling with this.' Teachers who don't seem interested in you. Teachers who tell you that you're behind and you'll have to work extra hard to catch up. Shouting.
Homework	Lots of homework. Endless assignments so you can never unwind, even at the weekends and over the holidays. Fights with parents about doing homework.
Sensory experiences	Everything seeming too much. Lights, noise and smells all feeling very intense and overwhelming.
No choices	Lack of time to follow your interests. No choices about what you learn or when you learn it. No time to do things that interest you.
Feeling not good enough	Feeling you are never doing well enough and should always be doing better. Being told you must try harder.
Academic pressure	Finding academic work hard and everything going too fast. Feeling that you are always falling behind and will never catch up.
Boredom	Finding much of your life tedious and boring but having to sit through it anyway. Finding academic work easy but you have to go through it all anyway.
Transitions	Spending your day going from room to room, so you never have time to settle into anything.
Fear and anxiety	Worries about getting into trouble (even if you have never been in trouble). Worries about being put on the spot. Worries about what your parents might do if they found out you've been in trouble.
Family arguments	Parents or other family members fighting. Parents trying to make you do things you don't want to do.
Bereavement	Losing someone important to you is really difficult and can take a long time to recover from.
Worries about money	Many people have been more worried about money and paying for things in the past few years. You might not have the money you need to buy things for yourself, or you're worried your parents don't have enough money to pay for the things your family needs.

Make your own list of the things wearing you down, the things you've been ignoring or trying to pretend don't really bother you, even really small things. Everything can add up. The route to burnout is usually one of lots of little things accumulating, rather than one big thing.

It doesn't matter whether someone else thinks something is important or not – what matters is whether it feels significant to you.

Doing this exercise might be really hard and you might get upset. You're going back over some of the hardest things in your life and you're allowing yourself to admit just how hard you found it all. If you have someone who would do it with you, it might be helpful, because it could stir up lots of thoughts and feelings.

Kaitlyn's Story

Kaitlyn was fourteen and she'd been out of school for eight months when she did this exercise with her mum. She didn't have worries about her home and parents, but she had found school extremely difficult. She and her mum realised that the hardest things about school for her had been other people bullying her, the academic work pressure and the anxiety of getting into trouble. She was someone who found Mathematics hard and never quite seemed to catch up. The other kids had noticed and called her Slow Coach, which she hated. Once one of the teachers had called her that too and she had had to stay at break to finish an exercise. Kaitlyn felt so ashamed and dreaded her parents finding out. Kaitlyn had never been in trouble but she dreamt about it every night and found it hard to sleep. Doing this exercise was really emotional for both Kaitlyn and her mum and Kaitlyn started crying as she remembered. It was still hard for her to tell her mum what had happened. Her mum hadn't realised that Kaitlyn felt so bad about this subject and she didn't know that other people called her names because of it.

While you have an honest look at your list, you can ask yourself if there is anything you can change about the things making life so stressful for you. Some things you might be able to change, but others you might not. You won't be able to change things that happened in the past, but you might be able to change how things work in the future.

Exercise: What Can I Change?

It can be helpful sometimes to divide things up into things you can change and things you can't change, so you can put your energy into the things you can change. Sometimes, when there are lots of difficult things in your life, you can feel overwhelmed by all the things you have to do. Dividing things up into those you can change and those you can't might help you feel more hopeful.

Make a list of the things that have been bothering you most and then ask yourself, is this something that could change? If so, how? If it can't change, how can I get more support with it?

Here are some examples from Kaitlyn, whom you read about above.

Stressful things	Can I change it? If so, what's the first step?	If I can't change it right now, is there a way to help manage it?
Boredom	Yes. I could make more time to do things that interest me. First step, talk to Mum or Dad about how to get some more interesting games to play.	
Granddad is really ill and I'm worried about him.	No. I can't make him well.	I could talk to Dad about how I feel and go to visit Granddad.
Friendship drama, they keep kicking me out of the groups online.	I can't change how they behave. I've told them it upsets me but they keep doing it.	I can switch off notifications so I don't see it all the time. I could join something in the evenings so I meet some new friends who aren't from school.

Feeling pressure to go back to school.	Yes. I could look at other ways to learn for now and ask my parents to stop telling me that if I don't go back to school ASAP I'll never get a job.	

When it comes to changing how things are at school, some schools are much more flexible than others. Some will allow you to take fewer exams, for example, or to work on your own sometimes rather than always sitting in class. Some will even let you come in part time and make up work at home. Others say you have to do everything and there's no middle ground. If your school is like this, you might need to talk to your parents about moving school or learning in other ways.

Amelia's Story

I dropped out of many different schools. In each school, I was bullied. I sometimes found myself in conflict with teachers, and I came home every day exhausted and overstimulated. I dreaded school and often refused to go. Most adults insisted to my mother that I *must* go to school, otherwise I wouldn't become 'properly socialised'. No one knew that I was autistic.

I dropped out of school before the end of sixth grade (ages 11–12) at the seventh school I'd attended. I had significant social difficulties, and I couldn't cope with chaotic school environments. I developed a stress-induced illness (irritable bowel syndrome) and spent the following year recovering at home.

I'm now a thirty-six-year-old philosophy professor, although I'm currently transitioning careers (I'm preparing to work with kids at a self-directed learning centre!). After I dropped out of sixth grade, I read lots of books, sang in a local choir and even learned a little bit of Latin. When I was thirteen, I had the opportunity to take a Latin course at a local university, which I loved. I gradually took more university courses, until I became a full-time university student at age fifteen. I went on to graduate school [university for people who have already got their first degree] at nineteen and got my first job working at a university when I was twenty-six. I still don't have a high-school diploma!

If I could go back, I would tell my teenage self, 'You will receive heaps of well-intended advice – but not all of it applies to you. You need to be on your own path, which falls far outside of most people's experiences. And most people *fear* things they have no experience with, which is why they fear for your future. Listen carefully to the advice people offer you. But if a piece of advice doesn't make sense – like, *really* make sense – let it go.' I would also tell her, 'Standardised tests are garbage.'

Amelia Hicks, associate professor of philosophy,
Kansas State University

When you're doing this, you might realise you are only doing some things because other people want you to, and actually you don't enjoy many of the things you do each day. When you spend your days being told what to do, sometimes you can forget what it is like to be making choices based on what *you* actually want.

What do You Need to Make Life Worth Living?

We've talked a lot about how to recover – but you want more than just recovery. You want to feel really good, to feel your life is enjoyable and stimulating. You want to be interested in life again.

Research shows us there are three core psychological needs that set the foundations for being psychologically well. These are:

1. Feeling that you are in the driving seat and have some control over your life.

2. Feeling that you can do things well and have a purpose in life.

3. Feeling that other people get you and have your back.

It's like you're driving your own vehicle and can choose where you go. You feel good about your driving skills and your ability to read the map, and you're with other people who love you and support you.

When people have these three things, they feel better about their life and are motivated to learn new things, even hard things. This is more than just being in the Zone, it's like a super-optimal Zone. Remember the recipe for burnout? This is the opposite of a recipe for burnout. It's an antidote.

The Burnout Antidote

Being in the driving seat of your life + purpose + supportive relationships = Burnout antidote

This is the fuel that keeps your vehicle going.

It's weird that more people don't understand this. Adults often assume that the reason people do things is because of money, or

because they are forced to do them. They say things like, 'Well, no one likes work (or school).' That's not actually true. Some people do like work (and school), and a lot of the difference is whether those three needs are met for them. Even tedious jobs can be fulfilling if you feel that you're in control, that you are good at your job and you like your colleagues.

When Naomi finished school she got a job in a cake factory. They paid her £3.50 an hour. She had to stand at a conveyor belt putting strawberries and kiwi slices onto cakes from 9 a.m. until 6 p.m., five days a week. In this job, she had almost no control over what she did. She had to stand in the same place until the supervisor, Dell, told her to move. Dell decided when it was Naomi's break time and lunch time. Naomi couldn't talk to anyone else because the cakes came down the belt too fast. They played terrible music all the time.

Even though she was really motivated at first, because she wanted to go travelling and she needed to earn the money, she only lasted three and a half weeks. None of her psychological needs were met there, except the need for purpose. Her purpose was to earn money – but that wasn't enough. Naomi had no control over what she did, she didn't feel she was doing it well and she couldn't talk to anyone. She started to feel terrible. At home, Naomi's head was full of imaginary pictures of cakes coming down conveyor belts. She couldn't stop worrying about missing a cake or dropping a kiwi. She had no energy for anything else.

Naomi was lucky; she got offered a job at a coffee shop instead and she left the cake factory. There she could talk to colleagues and customers and sometimes she managed to make a properly frothy cappuccino and felt good about it (sometimes she made a flat cappuccino and the customers complained, but that's another story . . .). The coffee shop was better. She could stick it out until she had saved enough money.

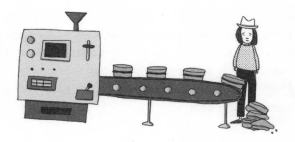

Think about your life. Where in your life do you feel in control and that you have a sense of purpose? Lots of teenagers tell me they feel best when playing *Minecraft* or *Fortnite*, doing a quest in *Dungeons and Dragons*, writing their own code for a game, or playing sports or music. Then they tell me that they don't have much time to do those things anymore because of the pressure of school, and so they have stopped. It's often the things we enjoy most that get cut when life is pressured, because we do those things for no other reason than enjoyment.

If you do nothing in your life where your psychological needs are met, you are not going to feel good about your life and the world. These are psychological **needs**, they are not 'nice to have' or 'a luxury'. Without them, we start to feel that life has no sparkle. We can push on through for a time, but it takes a toll on us. Burnout becomes more likely.

If you don't have many things in your life that make you feel good about yourself, think back. Was there a time when you did something that made you feel good about yourself? What was it? Could you try that again?

Exercise: Your Burnout Antidote

There are three elements to the burnout antidote, and you need to spend time doing all three of them to help keep you in the Zone. Writing them down (or drawing them or recording them in some other way) can help you remember and prioritise them.

Burnout antidote ingredients	What are the things you do that help you feel this way?	How could you make more space for this?
Feeling in the driving seat of your life		
Feeling that you are capable and are doing things that have meaning for you		
Feeling supported by other people who get you		

Here are some things teenagers tell us they do as part of their Burnout Antidote. These are things that help them to feel in control, capable and connected to others – the magic trio you need for the antidote.

Video games
Writing songs
Trampolining
Creating art
Writing novels

Playing chess or other complicated board games
Playing sports
Painting and rearranging their room
Coding
Learning a language
Learning a musical instrument
Doing puzzles
Diving into a passion or interest, no matter what it is
Singing in a choir
Getting fit
Reading books they love
Writing poetry
Acting in a play
Writing a play
Cooking
Swimming
Sorting their room out
Hanging out with friends
Designing and making clothes for themselves
Learning how to do stage makeup
Riding horses and mucking them out
Looking after pets
Singing songs from musicals
Modelling with polymer clay
Writing their story

A Quick Recap

As you start to feel better, it's time to think about what you need in your life. There's a lot of research showing that humans need three things in order to thrive. They are: feeling in control of (at least some aspects) your life; feeling that you are capable; and feeling connected to other people.

Lots of teenagers say they don't have those things at school and they only feel that way when doing things out of school. But they've had to stop doing things out of school because there is no time. Doing things that help you feel in control, which give you a purpose and a sense of connection are not just 'nice to haves'. They are really important for your wellbeing.

Creating your burnout antidote means making time for the things that help you to feel good about yourself and connected with other people. There are lots of different things this could include.

9

The Road Ahead

Stage 4: The Road Ahead

Okay, so don't jump to this section. Go back and do the earlier parts
first. If you are like most teenagers we meet, everyone is asking you
(pressuring you?) about what you're going to do next and how you
are going to get 'back on track'. Maybe you feel you can't recover
until you know what you're going to do. That's an illusion. It's one
of those burnout traps we talked about earlier – you can't get better
until you know what you'll do next, but you can't know what to do
next until you get better.

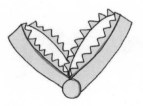

Firstly, you need to give yourself the space and time to decompress
and start to feel like yourself again. You need to lift the pressure off
to give yourself space to recover.

Next, when you do start to feel better, there's a danger. It's that
everyone around you will get very excited and start muttering about
going back to school and doing those exams and catching up. They
haven't quite understood that burnout isn't a problem with you – it's
your reaction to an environment that was not right for you. If you
go back into the same environment without any changes, it's likely

that the same thing will happen again. It might take some time and, meanwhile, everyone thinks everything is okay again, but, ultimately, burnout is a signal from your brain and body. It's saying STOP.

This means you need to think carefully about the next stage in your life and how you're going to build in the right road checks and maintenance, so that whatever you do next is sustainable.

This might mean having some hard conversations and also some soul-searching for your parents. They may have had ideas about you achieving certain exam results or going to university to study a particular subject. It also might involve a discussion in which all of you talk about where things went wrong, and how you could stop that happening again.

There are more options than you think. Most teenagers believe they have to be at school to do exams and go on to college, but that isn't strictly true. Some people do exams out of school, or they do exams through a school but don't attend classes, they study at home. Others decide that they don't want to do exams when everyone else does them. There are colleges that will take you without any exam passes, where you can study something while doing English and Mathematics alongside. You can study with the Open University or another online provider, and you don't necessarily need qualifications to do that. Sometimes, you can get an apprenticeship or start off volunteering and then get work off the back of that.

Often, when you've been through burnout, you get totally bogged down in how terrible you feel, and how many different pressures you feel. Now is the time for something different. It's the time to think to yourself about what you would like to be doing a few years in the future.

Lauren's Recovery

Lauren had been out of school for a year before she started to feel ready to think about what might happen next. Things had been hard for Lauren all the way through secondary school, but they had really gone wrong for her after her Year 9 exams. She got really stressed and vomited in an exam. Everyone had to be evacuated while they held their noses. She was so embarrassed. One of her 'friends' posted about it in their WhatsApp group with rows of vomit emojis and her name.

When she got home, she went to bed and hardly got up for the next week. When she did get out of bed, she could not face going

---

back to school. She felt numb and exhausted and her muscles ached like she had been really ill. The doctor said there was nothing wrong and she should go back to school, but when she tried she felt dizzy and fainted. Her dad had to come and pick her up. She lay around at home, feeling terrible. She watched daytime TV and slept. That phase lasted a few weeks, during which time her parents didn't pressure her to go back to school but spent time with her watching films together when they weren't at work. Her older sister was at college, so she was around a bit during the day and sometimes they played games together.

Lauren started to feel alive again through her pets. She had two cats and three guinea pigs. She would spend hours playing with the cats and lying with the guinea pigs on her chest. Then she started to design obstacle courses for her pets and see if she could train them to do mazes. She started to run a pet-feeding service in her neighbourhood when people were on holiday. She got to know all the local pets. She started to get interested in animal care and would watch videos of animal rescue centres. She found a book about animal psychology, which fascinated her. She started to be interested in the world again.

When Lauren got to the stage of looking back, she felt she had almost been a different person before all this happened. She had been so stressed about exams, and fitting in and what her friends would think. Now it all seemed far away, and when she was with the animals she felt calm. They didn't care what her exam results were. She could see that the school environment had been very stressful for her. Spending so much time with animals gave her an understanding of what they found stressful and how they reacted, and she felt that this helped her understand herself better.

Lauren decided she wanted to work with animals. She thought about going back to school, but when she talked to her friends, she could see it would mean just going right back into the same situation. There was no option to do fewer exams or go part time. Instead, she started to look at local colleges and discovered to her surprise that at the local agricultural college she could start a vocational animal management course when she was fourteen and could do Mathematics and English alongside it. However, she decided that she'd rather wait until she was sixteen to go to college. She first wanted to spend a couple of years building up her pet-sitting business and learning other things that interested her before going back into the world of assignments and assessments, even though college would be different to school. She started volunteering at the local cat rescue and made some new friends there. She worked towards an Arts Award and did some short courses online. When she did start college, she felt ready to study again and did well in her exams.

Creating Your Road Map

You don't need to have all the answers about what you want to do in the future – and you don't have to think years ahead. Just let yourself think about what you enjoy doing and what you'd like to do more of. What activities bring you alive?

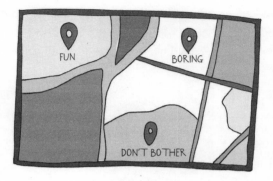

Sometimes people find it helpful to ask themselves a series of questions to break down what they might want to do. It might be helpful to talk to someone you trust about these questions if you get stuck.

Exercise: Writing Your Road Map

Where am I now?	
Where do I want to get to?	
What will I need to do to get there?	
What would be the first step in that direction?	
How can I take that first step?	
What might prevent me from taking that step (and how can I stop that from happening?)	
Who can I ask to help me with this?	

This doesn't have to be about big things in the future. You might just identify that you'd like to be spending more time with other people, or you'd like to improve your singing, or you'd like to become a better artist. The idea is that you break this down into small steps, so you can start and so your goals don't feel too big and unmanageable.

When you've done this exercise and have some idea about a direction you might want to go in, the next thing is to begin making the changes that will take you in the direction you want to go.

Even if you can't start right away, spend some time thinking about it. What will need to change for you to start living the life you want? What would be a first, tiny step taking you in the direction you want to go? Maybe you are sleeping a lot in the day and need to start waking up earlier so you could get a part-time job or join a class. Or maybe you'd like to be reading more books and you need to join the library and then visit it regularly.

It doesn't matter what it is, the task you have ahead of you is to make a change. This isn't easy. Lots of adults struggle with change. They do the same thing all the time, even if they don't really want to, because it's so hard to change.

Starting to Change

Changing things in your life can be hard and overwhelming. It's easy to start thinking about it and then get scared – or not know where to start. Or, it's easy to feel there is a huge gap between where you want to be and where you are right now.

There's a secret to this. It's a secret to almost all behavioural change if you want to make it stick. Lots of people make New Year's resolutions but they've given them up by 10 January. They start off so well, exercising for hours and getting up early each morning, but it doesn't last. That is typical for any sort of dramatic change. It works for a while and then you lose momentum.

You need another approach.

Here's the secret: Start Small, Make it Easy and Attractive, and Repeat. You could use the mnemonic SEAR to help you remember. Make sure it's SEARed into your memory. (We know that's a bit corny but it took us hours to come up with it.)

Let's say you want to get fit and your aim is to start to exercise. You feel completely overwhelmed by the idea of doing thirty minutes at the gym, plus you'd have to pay to go to the gym and go through an induction, and maybe you can only go if your parent takes you. And so every day you think you'll start tomorrow. You never start. You have such good intentions but it never happens.

Small

Instead of that, start small. Decide that you will go running for two minutes today. Just two minutes and then you'll come home. Or, you'll run on the spot in your front room. Then you'll do it again tomorrow. Just two minutes. You'll keep on doing two minutes until you feel you'd like to up it to three or even four.

Easy

The next step is to make it easy. Make it so easy to do the thing you want to do that it's easier to do than not to do it.

There are ways to trick yourself into doing things, and the main way is to make an earlier decision that makes it more likely that you will do that thing.

Naomi makes it easy for herself to exercise by getting up and putting on her running clothes immediately, first thing in the morning. Now she has created the expectation that she'll go running and she's made it easy for herself. She's also made it harder for herself not to go running, because she keeps reminding herself of running because of her clothes – and she doesn't want to be taking off her running clothes at the end of the day having not gone running. When she gets to the afternoon and is still wearing her running clothes, her family start to ask her if she's going running – which also reminds her to go.

Attractive

How can you make it fun to do the thing you want to start doing? What could you do so that you look forward to doing it? Could you listen to your favourite music while you exercise, or buy yourself your favourite cereal to wake up for?

Repeat

Keep doing that little, easy thing. Each day. The trick is to do it every day, even if you don't feel like it. In fact, it's most important on the days that you don't feel like it. But if you don't do it one day, don't catastrophise. All is not lost. Just do it the next day.

When it starts to get *really* easy or boring, make it just a little bit harder. Add an extra minute or two of exercise or get up a few minutes earlier.

This technique can be applied to pretty well anything and it can be a really useful way to start making changes when you feel there's a huge gap between where you are and where you'd like to be. The size of the gap can stop you from ever getting started, so this technique is like building a series of tiny bridges, each taking you a bit nearer to where you want to be.

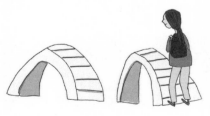

Quitting can be a Good Thing

We've been talking about how to get your life going again, and how to make changes so you can start doing things you want to do and which are important to you. However, there's one really important skill you'll need to practise if you want to protect yourself from burnout in the long term. Quitting.

What comes into your mind when you hear the word 'quitting'? Teenagers tell us it makes them think things like 'loser', 'never get anywhere', 'can't stick at anything'. Quitting has a PR problem. Most people think it means something bad.

Most teenagers are told at some point that they shouldn't quit something. You might have been told you have to continue with swimming lessons, even if the teacher shouts, or you have to keep playing sports on Saturday mornings because otherwise you are letting the rest of the team down.

You might even have seen 'inspirational' memes saying things like, 'Quitters Never Win, and Winners Never Quit' (Vince Lombardi) or 'Never Quit Trying'. Our culture puts a lot of emphasis on not quitting and is often derogatory about those who decide to quit.

All of these messages can make you feel that you can't stop doing something, even if you really don't like it or it makes you feel ill. It can make you feel like you are stuck in a trap – either you continue to do something you dislike, or you become a 'quitter' or a 'loser'.

None of it is true. People quit things all the time – and being a winner often means quitting other things in order to focus. If you talk to someone who is a successful athlete or musician, they will tell you all the things they had to quit in order to concentrate on their sport or music. Piano players quit playing football in case they damage their hands, while some young people quit all extra-curricular activities in order to focus on playing tennis or ice-skating. Young actors sometimes quit school so they can spend their time in the theatre or on a film set. They learn in other ways.

The idea that you shouldn't quit is particularly unhelpful for young people, because it prevents you from being able to try things out. Being a teenager is the perfect time to experiment with lots of different ways of being and doing – and in order to experiment, you have to be able to quit. If you know that you can't quit, it can feel too scary even to try something out, as you might end up committed for months or even years.

Your parents might say to you that you can't quit something because they have paid for you to do it and they can't afford for you to quit. They may feel that this is true, but actually it isn't quite true. They can afford to pay for you because they already have. The money is gone whether you do the activity or not. The choice is only whether you do the activity or not.

Sometimes the 'no quitting' mantra can be used to make people do things they really don't want to do. It can be a way of bullying people. Then you might feel trapped – and that puts you at risk of burnout. This is what happened to Arthur.

Arthur's Story

Arthur was a skilled musician and played in a regional youth orchestra while also having music lessons. He had played the trumpet since he was eight and had been passionate about it. When he was thirteen, he started to enjoy it a bit less and also wanted to have more time to hang out with his friends and play sport. He suggested to his music teacher that he might stop going to the orchestra. His music teacher responded by saying that she hadn't thought he was a quitter and she was disappointed in him. She said that she thought he had great potential but he wouldn't ever fulfil it if he just gave up and spent time with his friends.

He mentioned it to his dad who said that the youth orchestra was very prestigious and he was lucky to be in it. He said that if Arthur quit this time, he wouldn't get into the national youth orchestra for older teenagers and so it would be a permanent decision that could affect his whole future. Arthur felt trapped. Both his dad and his music teacher said they wouldn't stop him from quitting – but they also made it clear that they thought it would reflect badly on him if he did. He kept going to orchestra but he stopped enjoying it. What had been a joy became a chore. He didn't feel that he had a choice.

Quitting something can be one of the most important things you do in your life. Naomi quit studying medicine after two years. It wasn't an easy decision and part of her wondered if she was 'giving up' or 'taking the easy way out'. It's true that that decision meant she'll never be a doctor. You could say it stopped her from 'winning' at medicine.

However, it was the right decision for her and it opened up the opportunity to be a psychologist instead. She has also quit several jobs which weren't right for her, often quite quickly after only a few weeks. She knows the signs now telling her she needs to quit – prickly skin, brain fog, lethargy and trouble relaxing. She knows it's better to quit before things get worse, as otherwise it can take her a long time to recover.

Quitting Myths	Quitting Truths
Winners never quit.	Winners quit many things.
Giving up is the easy option.	Giving up can be the right option and often isn't at all easy.
Quitters never win.	Quitting something can open up the opportunity for you to 'win' elsewhere. Life isn't all about winning.
Quitting becomes a habit if you do it.	Quitting in itself isn't a habit. Deciding whether something works for you can be a habit – and a good one.
Failure is temporary but quitting is permanent.	Quitting does not have to be permanent. You can quit something at one point and then decide to start again later.
Quitting is not an option.	Quitting should always be an option, otherwise you are trapped.

Are there any other myths you've been told about quitting? You could write them down and see whether you think they are really true. Most of them sound true, but when you really think about them, you realise that they aren't true at all. Just because people say something many times doesn't make it true.

As you are recovering from burnout, knowing that you can quit and feel good about that is really important. It is so much easier to try things out when you know that you can stop if you want to. Part of burnout recovery is learning your limits, and this will be a really useful skill for the future. Deciding when to quit and when to keep going is a skill for life – and the only way you'll get a chance to find your own limits is by trying things out, knowing that you can stop when you want to.

Here are some alternatives we have come up with.

Alternative Quitting Beliefs

Knowing when to quit is a strength.

Closing one door means another can open.

Quitting is an art that needs practising like any other.

Quitting is the process of deciding how to prioritise your time and energy.

Quit while you're still ahead.

The best time to quit is before you have no choice but to do so.

Winners are quitters too.

Are there any other alternative quitting beliefs you think would be useful? Maybe you can design some 'inspirational' memes of your own with images, to encourage people to quit before they burn out. Or you could make your own propaganda posters and stick them around your home. Maybe other people in your family could benefit from quitting some things that aren't working for them.

Growing up is a process of finding out what works for you. You don't have to have everything worked out as a teenager, even if people tell you that you do. You don't have to know what your identity will be, you don't have to know what your 'true self' really is. You can explore and try things out, and along the way you will make mistakes and you'll decide to quit things. Keeping the option open to quit and make changes is a strength, not a weakness.

Things Will Go Up and Down

Change takes a while, and often it can feel like things get worse *and* better. You really want to feel better every day, but actually some days you just feel terrible and can't do anything.

That is part of recovery. Everyone goes through this. It is never straightforward or easy. If someone promises an easy, effortless change, be suspicious; they are probably trying to sell you something. You might think you're doing really well and then you have a hard week and feel like you're back to square one.

You're not. Getting better isn't a straight line. It's more like an obstacle course. Over time, you will progress and things will improve, but you might not be able to see that until you look back.

You are learning new ways to manage yourself and your life. You're learning what environments work for you – and how you might need to make choices to create the environments that work for you. You're also learning what you need to feel good and keep yourself moving forwards. All those things are really important and the things you learn will last you a lifetime. You will look back on this time and see it as the time when you found you had to reset everything – when you discovered it was possible to take different routes through life.

There is more than one way to live and learn.

A Quick Recap

The fourth stage of burnout recovery is when you start to look at and plan the way ahead. You've already looked behind yourself and worked out where things went wrong, and now this is about thinking about what is important to you going forward.

Making changes can be hard, and we've suggested a way to start to make small changes in your life. We've also talked about thoughts that can make it more difficult to make changes, such as the idea that you shouldn't quit things. Not feeling that you can quit can make it impossible to start anything new, as you might get trapped.

You don't have to know what you are going to do in the future to start to plan your way forward. It's fine to work it out as you go along and plan things one step at a time. Everyone needs time to try things out and then change their mind. Deciding that something isn't for you isn't a failure.

The road to recovery is never smooth. There will always be ups and downs, which is understandable. Those ups and downs don't mean you aren't getting better. You are making a new path for yourself and that is never easy.

Ending

We've come a long way in this book. We're talked about burnout, school and why people burn out. You've heard lots of our stories about our experiences, along with stories about the experiences of others. We've made some suggestions for how you might get yourself on the road to recovery.

We've used the metaphor of a motor vehicle and the road to talk about how to recover from burnout. There are four stages and you will want to think about how they might apply in your life. In the Breakdown phase, what you need is to turn down the pressure. In the Repair stage, you need to begin doing things you enjoy. Then you can start looking behind you and making sense of what happened. And then, only at the end of the process, is it time to think about your future and where you want to get to – and how you might start to do it. One of the exercises in this book is to make a roadmap to plan for your future.

You can't get better alone, and you can't just go back to how things were before. Burnout is about the environment around you and how it affects you. You need the support of others to help you create a better future for yourself, one that suits you. One of the first things to do is to identify who might be able to help you – and then ask them. You could show them this book to get the conversation started.

We hope the book will give you some hope for your future and will help you to see that you are not alone in feeling the way you do. Many thousands of young people have similar experiences and they have found a way forwards. Each person's path will be different and we can't tell you what will be right for you. We hope that you might be starting to get excited about finding your way – or at least, just seeing that there might be a path out of the way you are feeling right now.

A Guide to Teenage Burnout for Adults

About This Book

Most books for teenagers who are distressed by or not attending school focus on how to get them back into school. There is often the assumption that if a teenager returns to school, this will be their route to emotional wellbeing and future happiness. To this end, a significant amount of pressure is often applied, and books sometimes take the approach of persuading young people that school really isn't as bad as they think it is. Books for parents tell them to put incentives (and disincentives) in place to ensure that their teenager attends school regularly, no matter what they say.

This book is different. It puts mental health and emotional wellbeing first. It encourages teenagers to think about themselves and the things they need in life to be happy – and to ask themselves whether school provides that. For this reason, you as an adult might find the contents of the book quite challenging. It is upfront about the reasons the school system can cause distress in young people. It does not try to persuade them that school isn't as bad as they think. It starts with validating young people's experiences.

The reason for this is that our experience working with teenagers indicates that they do not need more people telling them how important school is and how it's a good thing. Teenagers tell us that everyone tells them this, and it makes them feel pressured and anxious. They lose hope in the future, because they are told that their only chance to get a fulfilling job and an interesting life is to do well at school, and yet, for many of them, school is a struggle. The whole premise of this book is that burnout recovery needs to start with lifting pressure and making space to recover – and teenagers can't do that while they are being pressured to return to life as it was before. We hope this book will enable teenagers (and their parents) to think critically about school, and to appreciate the good while acknowledging the ways in which it hasn't been working for them.

What's Going On?

There are signs that school is not working for an increasing number of young people. Over the past few years, more and more teenagers are showing the signs of chronic stress and burnout that were previously mostly seen in adults. Some of them stop doing almost everything and spend their lives mostly in their bedrooms. This can be really frightening for their families. It's hard to understand what is going on.

The reasons for this behaviour will be different for each individual. However, there are some factors this generation is managing that are unique to them. The past few years included a global pandemic, several wars, and reports of climate breakdown and disaster. It has been hard to be optimistic about the future. In particular, two years of pandemic with a high degree of uncertainty, anxiety and separation from other people have taken their toll on many young people. In addition, this generation of young people are exposed to an unprecedented amount of social pressure and social comparison via the internet, and for some this causes very high anxiety.

While every age group experienced the pandemic, there are reasons to think that it may have had a greater psychological impact on children and adolescents than adults. Children have a shorter life experience, and the things that happen in childhood tend to affect the way we learn to think and feel about the world. During the pandemic, many children learnt that the world around them wasn't safe and that the only way to protect themselves was to stay at home and stay two metres away from other people. Many of them developed anxieties about handwashing or contamination with germs. In addition, they were prevented from spending time with other people their own age and were not able to take the usual developmental steps towards independence. For some young people, it was the first time they realised that their parents couldn't fix everything. It's not surprising many became more anxious during that period.

Some schools have made great efforts to help young people recover their sense of wellbeing and to rebuild communities. On a national level, however, the focus after the pandemic was very much on academic catch-up, with media reports that this generation was 'behind'. There was very little emphasis on the social and emotional effects of those two years and no emphasis on catching up on lost play. Schools were 'back to normal' – except that many young people found that they could not return to normal. Teachers reported increased rates of persistent absenteeism and behavioural problems. At the same time, many schools introduced high-pressure strategies to improve exam results. These strategies often increase anxiety and the pressure placed on young people and reduce the amount of choice they have in their lives. Some young people get stuck in a downward spiral of detentions and isolation, and this can quickly lead to burnout.

What is Burnout?

When humans are under a lot of pressure for a sustained period of time, they can become chronically stressed – and chronic stress can lead to burnout. Burnout is defined by the World Health Organization (WHO) as an occupational phenomenon, characterised by feelings of negativity, fatigue and loss of energy and a sense of not being able to do things well. The WHO says that burnout is a result of a mismatch between the demands on a person, and the resources they have available to them. Some young people are susceptible to burnout because their school environment is particularly ill-suited to them. Some of these young people will be identified as neurodivergent, while others will not. The appropriate response to burnout is to look at changing the environment, rather than the person.

For many young people, it seems that the demands of the last few years have exceeded their ability to cope, and they find themselves unable to continue with life as usual. Because one way in which they show this is through difficulties with attending school, they are often treated punitively by the school system and their families. Their reluctance is seen as their fault and they are told they must try harder. This exacerbates the problem because it puts them under more stress and pressure.

Many young people blame themselves when things go wrong, which also makes their stress worse. This prevents them from recovering. The approach outlined in this book is to help young people locate the problem in things outside themselves, and to see their burnout as an outcome of an environment that isn't working for them, rather than as a weakness in themselves. For this reason, it encourages young people to reflect on the way they interact with their environment, and on what works for them and what doesn't. This process can be challenging for parents! It may mean that young people are very negative about their school experiences when you think this isn't justified. It may help to see this as part of their process of working out what has gone wrong, so that they can start to see a future for themselves.

Autistic Burnout

Recently some people have started to talk about 'autistic burnout' as something which is different to burnout in non-autistic people. Many autistic people do experience burnout and they may be particularly vulnerable. However, there is no evidence that the process of burnout is distinctly different in autistic people, nor that they need to do something different in order to recover. Most of the young people Naomi works with are autistic, and the approach described in this book is inclusive of neurodiversity.

Can School Really Lead to Burnout?

Many parents are sceptical that school could lead to burnout. After all, they think, everyone goes to school and we all got through it. There have always been young people who have found the school environment affected them badly, but in previous generations this was understood in medical or behavioural terms – teenagers were signed off school with glandular fever or were labelled as truants or school refusers. This generation is more aware of mental health and, hence, the way we think about it is as burnout. It's also true that school has become more pressured, with more high-stakes testing from early on. It is common for teenagers to be told that their whole life depends on how well they do at school. Many of them feel trapped and unhappy and can't see a way out.

Part of this journey of recovery for your teenager may include you reflecting on your own path through education and how it affected you, both negatively and positively. Many parents find that they start questioning the assumptions about school and education they've held since childhood. Some of these assumptions are listed in Chapter 3. Perhaps the most important one for parents is that school is not the only way to get an education. If your child can't return to school, it does not have to be the end of their hopes and dreams. There are other ways to learn. They may be less convenient and harder to find, but they are there. Just knowing that school is not the only way can make the difference for a teenager. When they no longer feel trapped, the world can open up.

What Can We Do?

What's your role? It's very hard when your child is in burnout. You may well feel highly anxious and be desperate for them to get back on track. This pressure won't help them recover and can, in fact, keep them stuck – one of the 'burnout traps' described in the book.

If you start from the premise that the only possible outcome for your child is a return to regular school attendance, then you have already limited your chances of success. We know this is probably what you want and what everyone wants, but burnout is a reaction to the environment. Returning to the same environment is likely to cause the same problems again unless significant changes are made.

Think about it in terms of an adult at work. If an adult is experiencing burnout from a highly stressful job, we would never assume that the only possible way for them to recover is to return to that job. We'd be thinking about how they might be able to either talk to their boss and change how their job works or move job. Yet with burnt-out children and school, it's common to assume that a return to school-as-usual is the only really successful outcome.

One thing teenagers says consistently is that they feel trapped when everyone tells them there is no other way to live a good life except by doing well at school. This leads some of them to despair. This is why in this book we have so much focus on the things everyone says about school, but which may not be true. It's important for teenagers to know that even if their school experience is very difficult and they don't do well, they can still have a fulfilling future.

This means that part of the process of you and your child recovering from burnout may be to consider alternative educational pathways. Even if, in fact, your child does return to school, just thinking about the other options can lift some of the pressure off, which perversely makes it easier to go back, if that is what they want.

We've outlined a four-stage recovery pathway in this book. When teenagers are in burnout, there is often a lot of pressure for them to get back to school and studying as quickly as possible. This can actually prevent young people from getting better. They are already feeling pressured and adding more pressure won't help. Recognising which stage they are at can help you to adapt your expectations and approach.

The four stages of recovery are:

1. Breakdown
This is when everything goes wrong. Sometimes this can happen after a long build-up and at other times it seems to come out of the blue for parents. Something, sometimes quite a minor thing, happens and suddenly the teenager is no longer able to keep going with their life. It's as if they've got nothing left.

At this point, lifting off the pressure is crucial. Many parents try to be helpful by asking their teenager each day if they feel able to go to school, but this, in itself, can feel like pressure. Just agreeing that they will have a period of time off without reminders can help everyone relax, which creates the time and space for recovery. You might need to be your child's protector, preventing other people from applying the pressure.

When it comes to pressure, you need to be led by your teenager as to what feels like pressure. It's likely that they will have a different perspective on this to you. You might think you are being supportive and they think you are piling on the anxiety. At this point, just listen. Breakdown is not the stage to get into discussions about this or to take it personally. They are likely to be extremely sensitive (and, possibly, so are you).

At this stage, you want to focus on love and connection. Your teenager needs to know that your love for them is unconditional and that you value them just as they are. This might involve showing an interest in their video games or watching films with them. It could mean cooking their favourite food. If your teenager won't talk to you at all, you could think about whether they might find other people more approachable. Older siblings or relatives can feel like less of a pressure, or some people find mentors who come and do things with their children that they enjoy. Find people who can come and spend regular time with your child, even if this just involves sitting on the sofa next to them. They need to know that others care about them.

We've talked quite a bit about social media in this section of the book. In our experience, social media and WhatsApp groups can be an intense source of pressure for young people that they can't get away from. Adolescents are particularly vulnerable to social influence. Some teenagers develop new symptoms or think they might have different mental health problems as a result of what they see on social media. If your teenager is restricting their eating one month, then they develop tics and then the next month they say that they might have bipolar depression or dissociative identity disorder, then it is possible that they are being influenced by social media. This doesn't mean that they are doing this on purpose nor that the symptoms aren't a real sign of distress. If you think social media is having a negative effect on your teenager and is preventing them from finding the space they need to recover from burnout, you may need to step in and either stop them or monitor their communications. Talk to them about it first, don't go straight in with blanket bans, but also be prepared to act, if you are concerned. If you do decide to ban things, then don't just take things away but instead think about offering new opportunities. For example, if you think YouTube and TikTok are problematic for your child because of the content they are accessing, find some other streaming services they can access safely instead.

Breakdown is very difficult for parents. Your anxiety may be extremely high, as you see your child's life apparently falling apart around you.

It's common for parents to say that everything seemed to be going so well, that their child was a high achiever and always busy, and now overnight they won't leave their bedroom and it seems like all is lost.

It will make your child feel worse if you can't manage your own anxiety around them. Find people to talk to outside the family if you need them, people to whom you can express your own feelings about what is happening.

2. Repair

This is the stage where things have started to settle down a bit. There is a 'new normal', even if that new normal isn't one you wanted or are happy about. You might have had to rearrange things in your life to accommodate the reality that your child isn't attending school. You may even have had to give up work or rearrange your hours. Your child might be signed off sick. You aren't in immediate crisis anymore.

The aim of this stage is for your teenager to start to reconnect with what is important to them and their interests. When people are burnt out, they often feel like nothing is worth doing and nothing is enjoyable. They may have no idea what they want to do. The first sign of recovery is when they show an interest in doing something, even if that thing is going to the local shop to buy chocolate.

When they start to show signs of being interested in something again, you can encourage that without putting on pressure or jumping on it. This seems a bit counter-intuitive but it's really easy to squash these early signs of recovery by too much parental enthusiasm, which immediately feels pressuring. Support might involve facilitating new interests, which are often very different to school subjects and sometimes challenging for parents. Teenagers we know of have developed intense interests in horror films, lock-breaking and serial killers – perhaps as ways of pushing their parents' boundaries. You need to keep them safe at the same time as showing that you value the things they are interested in.

Keeping the pressure off is still crucial. It's easy to push a teenager back into Breakdown if you react to any signs of improvement by suggesting a return to school or by telling them that if they are well enough to do the things they enjoy, then they are well enough to do their homework. The likely outcome of saying this is that they will do neither the things they enjoy nor the homework.

3. Learning from the Journey

When your teenager is starting to engage with life again and you can see they are showing an interest in things and have regained some curiosity, then it might be time to start thinking about what went wrong. It can take months before a teenager is ready to do this.

We've suggested several exercises in this book that you could do with your child, but this is also something you can do for yourself. It can be helpful to identify your own beliefs about parenting and education that might have contributed to what has happened. For example, parents often tell us that they don't want to repeat the missed opportunities of their own childhood, and so go to huge lengths to encourage their children to do things like join a sports team or become a competitive chess player. For the child, this can feel like a pressure, while to the parent it feels like encouragement and support. This doesn't mean that it's your fault. You were doing the best you could, but you might need to change how you do that now.

For a parent, this can be a very emotional stage. It's possible that your teenager will tell you that things you have worked very hard for and have put a lot of time into were stressful for them. To continue with the driving metaphor, you may need to find a different road and decide to spend your energies differently. Some parents tell us that their child's burnout is the catalyst for a complete U-turn in their parenting style and they have dropped many of the things they held dear.

Again, finding support for yourself as you go through this is crucial. Your child is going through their own emotional process and they can't take on yours as well. Get out of the house (even if your child isn't doing the same), go and talk to friends and make space for your own feelings about the whole thing.

4. The Road Ahead

Finally, it's time to think about the future. It's so tempting to try and skip straight to this stage, but it will just feel like more pressure to your teenager and will push them further into burnout if you try it too soon.

There are lots of things in the chapter you could try for yourself or with your teenager; in particular, thinking about challenging your own assumptions about both school and quitting. The research shows that when young people get to the point of being unable to attend school, not all of them end up returning to regular attendance. Regular school attendance is one way to get an education, but there are other ways.

The worst situation for young people, in our experience, is to be stuck in limbo. They aren't attending school, but are also not being offered anything else and, sometimes, they're being told that they are not achieving anything and that they have no education. They feel constantly under pressure and unhappy, with any sign of improvement met with, 'How about school tomorrow?' This limbo is most likely to happen when everyone focuses on a return to school being the only possible outcome. We sometimes speak to parents who have been trying to get their children back into school for years without success. In that time, no other education has happened and everyone is unhappy. It dominates family life.

That's why this chapter focuses on helping teenagers think about a way forward, whether or not they return to school. Whatever the situation, you can help your teenager access new opportunities and talk positively about what they are learning. If they are really into video games, then they will be learning there. If their thing is digital art, amine or collecting objects, then they will be learning there. Showing them that you value their interests is one way to show them that you care about them. Find new opportunities for them to pursue those interests.

If it becomes clear that a return to school is not going to happen, then there are various ways in which teenagers can get an education outside school. Some parents deregister and home educate. In this case, they get no funding but are free to educate in whatever way works best for their child. Others get packages from the local authority, which gives them access to tutoring or specialist services. Others sign up for online courses or join programmes at local colleges, which are often very different to school.

For younger children, research with home-educated children indicates that it is not necessary to be doing much formal learning at all. Many decide to unschool, a method of home education that is entirely informal for as long as the child wants it to be this way. If this interests you, we have listed some books on the subject at the end.

Whatever you and your teenager decide, giving them some space free of pressure is the key, and this will involve thinking out of the box – dropping some exams, for example, even if they do return to school. The 'burnout antidote' described in the book is important. They need time to focus on the things they enjoy and which make them happy, whether or not they take qualifications or go back to school.

As their parent, you need to be a safe place to land. The most important thing is to help them to feel hopeful about the future again, no matter what path they end up taking. You want to be able to remember this time as a (difficult) period of re-evaluation and regeneration, rather than one of failure and despair.

If you can, find other families in a similar situation or those who are further down the line and who can give you some hope for the future. Your teenager can and will recover, but it won't happen overnight and their future may look different to what you had imagined for them. Holding on to hope and trusting in the process is what will keep you all going, and that takes a lot of emotional effort from parents. Think about what you need to keep yourself going. You need your own burnout antidote too.

What Approach Does This Book Take?

This book takes an eclectic approach – meaning that it draws on several different types of evidence-based therapeutic and psychological models. The main influences are acceptance and commitment therapy (ACT), polyvagal theory, self-determination theory and cognitive therapy.

Do we Need a Therapist?

If your teenager is very withdrawn and won't talk to you, then it can be hard to reach them. Finding other interested adults who can spend time with them can really help. These don't have to be therapists. Relatives who will come and just hang out could be really helpful, or family friends who will come and play video games or music. Young adults can sometimes make connections with teenagers more easily than to their parents. Think in terms of trying in increase the number of low-pressure social opportunities they have available to them. Therapy might come later, but it isn't always the answer, particularly if the young person themselves isn't the one driving the process. Meet any therapist first and explain to them your priorities for your child. Many therapists will assume that your goal will be a return to school and this can make any sessions unproductive.

What if We Need More Help?

Organisations Who May Be Able to Offer You Support and Information

Young Minds www.youngminds.org.uk
Not Fine In School notfineinschool.co.uk
Define Fine www.definefine.org.uk
Square Peg www.teamsquarepeg.org
National Autistic Society www.autism.org.uk
PDA Society www.pdasociety.org.uk

Alternatives to School

Progressive Education www.progressiveeducation.org
Alliance for Self-Directed Education www.self-directed.org

Books about Learning Outside School

For Teenagers
The Art of Self-Directed Learning: 23 Tips for Giving Yourself an Unconventional Education by Blake Boles

The Teenage Liberation Handbook: How to Quit School and Get a Real Life and Education by Grace Llewellyn

For Parents
Changing Our Minds: How Children Can Take Control of their Own Learning by Naomi Fisher
Free to Learn: How Unleashing the Instinct to Play will Make Our Children Happier, More Self-Reliant and Better Students for Life by Peter Gray

How Children Learn At Home by Alan Thomas and Harriet Pattison

Finding a Therapist
Qualified therapists should be registered with a professional body. This professional organisation will set ethical standards and regulate their practice. This means that if things go wrong, you will have someone to complain to.

There are many people who call themselves coaches but who are unregulated. People may also run programmes for teenagers that they claim will get teenagers back to school. Ask for their qualifications and the regulatory body they are a member of before signing up and watch out for unscrupulous companies making claims to transform you and your teenager's life. Anyone who is using a hard-sell approach is unlikely to be a qualified professional.

Psychfinder (For UK registered psychologists).
www.psychfinder.co.uk.

BABCP (For cognitive behavioural psychotherapists)
www.babcp.com

BACP (For counsellors and psychotherapists).
www.bacp.co.uk.

UKCP (For psychotherapists and psychotherapeutic counsellors).
www.psychotherapy.org.uk

EMDR Association (For EMDR therapists).
www.emdrassociation.org.uk

Index